CU00958633

LIFEBOATS OF THE HUMBER

by Barry Herbert

Hutton Press
1991

Published by the Hutton Press Ltd.
130 Canada Drive, Cherry Burton, Beverley
North Humberside HU17 7SB

Copyright © 1991

No part of this book may be reproduced, stored in a
retrieval system or transmitted in any form, or by any
means electronic, mechanical, photocopying, recording
or otherwise without the prior permission of the
Publisher and the Copyright holders.

Typeset and printed by
Image Colourprint Ltd.,
Anlaby, Hull.

ISBN 1 872167 17 9

CONTENTS

Acknowledgements 5

Foreword 6

Chapter One - Origins of the Cleethorpes and Grimsby Lifeboat Stations 1868-1927......... 7

Chapter Two - Lifeboats at Spurn Point 1810-1908 34

Chapter Three - Metamorphis 1908-1911 51

Chapter Four - The dawn of the RNLI era 69

Chapter Five - Power takes over 74

Chapter Six - Rescues 77

Chapter Seven - The Lifeboats 97

Chapter Eight - Three notable Coxswains 108

Chapter Nine - At last, a visit to Spurn 113

This book is dedicated to my Mother for her help and support in the researches and compilation of this manuscript.

ACKNOWLEDGEMENTS

For the Idea, Mr. Alan Fenner

Thanks for their help to:-

Paul Berriff, for his front cover photograph.

Ken Stevens, (Cleethorpes Branch RNLI).

Stuart Swallow, (RNLI Public Relations).

Brian Beckett, (Cleethorpes Vigilantes Rescue Association)

The late Captain E. Senior.

Barry Gee.

David Linklater, (RNLI) Poole.

Charles Ekberg.

Mrs. Jill Ward.

Brian Bevan, (Coxswain, Humber Lifeboat).

Ian Firman, (Assistant Coxswain Humber Lifeboat).

Grimsby Evening Telegraph.

Fred Sizer.

Captain D. C. Thomas.

Mr. E. Russell, (Hull Trinity House).

Mr. F. B. Robinson, for the Foreword.

Brian Salt.

Eric G. Cope.

Mr. A. Whitaker, (Bradford Telegraph and Argus).

Mr. W. Hobson.

Arthur Credland, Hull Town Docks Museum.

Malcolm Fussey, Alan Emmerson, Michael Ulyatt,

Peter Chapman, Jeff Wells, Michael Furness,

Mr. B. Major, and many others.

FOREWORD

Anyone browsing over this book seems likely to have an enquiring mind, and one that can only be satisfied by ultimately reading it.

On reading it, one will appreciate the depth of understanding and sympathetic treatment by the Author, Mr. Barry Herbert, for he not only achieves a good historical account of the River Humber Lifeboats, he not only describes the heroism by which many rescues have been achieved over the years, but also delves into the politics of operating the Service, originally by a set of people who graphically called themselves the Oddfellows, then in turn the R.N.L.I. (the Royal National Lifeboat Institution) enters the scene, and after a while, H.M. Government decreed that the Lifeboat operations on the River Humber should come under the umbrella of the Humber Conservancy Board based on Kingston upon Hull, but failed to provide financial means, and which the reader will find that, that too provides the stage for difficulties and arguments on which the Author does well in his espousal of the problems.

Above all however Barry does good justice to the many deeds of skill and bravery accomplished by those (Oddfellows) who undertook battling the elements under most difficult conditions of weather, tides, cross currents and the occasional freak wave that threatened both those who were wrecked and those attempting to help them and sometimes the boat(s) as well.

In my view, the story is competently written, and well worth reading.

I say this as one having experienced some 38 years in a family Trawling business, 25 years of which as managing director and part owner, plus 6 years in the Army during the 1939-45 war, 3 of which were in the Royal Engineers, Docks and Inland Water Transport, partly in Burma. Also for the last 25 years as a member of Lloyds, dealing in large part in underwriting Marine risks.

To the reader, happy reading.

F. B. Robinson.
February 1990

CHAPTER ONE

ORIGINS OF THE CLEETHORPES-GRIMSBY LIFEBOAT STATIONS 1868-1927

The Royal National Lifeboat Institution has its roots in the formation of a Lifeboat service first evolved by Colonel Sir William Hillary in 1824. Hillary lived in Douglas, Isle of Man and had seen many shipwrecks and had put his own life at risk to help to rescue over 300 people from death at sea.

In 1824, Sir William Hillary published an Appeal to the Nation to ask for funds and ideas to set up a rescue service to be offered on a 24 hours call basis nationwide.

The first title of this service was rather ponderous, it was named "The Royal National Institution for the Preservation of Life from Shipwreck". The present title was adopted in 1854. Hillary's enthusiasm and zest for life fired the imagination of many and the rescue movement grew gradually but very surely. Hillary was able to establish Lifeboat Stations on the Isle of Man and he won the Institution's Gold Medal for Gallantry 3 times for his service with the Douglas Lifeboat.

In 1824 there were already 39 serviceable lifeboats in existence in the British Isles; 25 were provided by Lloyds of London and the rest by local benefactors and public minded members of the Community plus interest from the Friendly Societies. The purpose built lifeboats had been used since the 1790's but there was a lack of organisation and cohesion missing from the early efforts to offer a rescue service, the number of lifeboats was inadequate to serve the increasing sea borne trade and this situation showed the need for a well organised National Rescue Service.

After an enthusiastic beginning the novelty began to wane and the Institution found itself in a decline. Money was proving difficult to obtain and in 1850 there were only 19 lifeboats associated with the Institution's Service. However, in the following year, things began to improve and at that time some 90 lifeboats were found to be in service, of which 30 were operated by the Institution, this figure further improved by 1869 when 200 boats were available and this total increased to 300 in 1891.

By 1891 most local lifeboats had acknowledged and supported the Institution to facilitate the work of the rescue operation.

During the period 1854-1869, the Institution received a Government Grant but this was relinquished at the Institution's request as the Government's imposed conditions proved very unpopular with the local Station's Committees, further more the availability of the Government Grant greatly affected the potential income from voluntary contributions.

In 1890, the first steam powered lifeboat was introduced for evaluation purposes, soon after that experiments were tried with internal combustion engines in 1904.

Progress was being made and the credibility of the Institution was growing strongly, the public's awareness and interest had been stirred and was very sympathetic to this rescue service and they gave generously in financial terms, thus enabling more lifeboats to be designed purposely for the job in hand.

However, much thought and development was to come before full satisfaction could be claimed, if ever, for the RNLI is an organisation that seeks to improve and develop all the time.

The yardstick to gauge the success of the rescue service were the rescues attempted and the lives saved. The lives saved column was growing gradually, depending on the nature of the rescue. The early days were certainly very adventurous and risks were taken that would be dismissed out of hand in the more knowledgable days. The RNLI was growing in confidence and its reputation for sound reliability was being broadcast through the branches that supported the operation. The public's knowledge about the RNLI was very important and the London Committee was most anxious to promote the 'right' kind of image of a reliable rescue service that was, and still is, self supporting, a remarkable achievement and a good solid foundation for the future.

The days before the coming of the lifeboat at Cleethorpes were ones of continued, but calculated risk. The fishing smacks had an average crew of 4 and in those far off times when a small fishing smack left port, it was quite reasonable to assume that the vessel and crew would never be seen again. Fortunately, perhaps 95% of the fishing fleet returned safely, laden with prime fish which was hard earned and hopefully realised enough money to sustain the owner and crew.

If any vessel got into difficulties, weather caused most of the problems. Fog and mist also brought situations that caused extreme caution and vigilance, collisions were frequent in such conditions, and there was always the risk of grounding on the many sand and gravel banks that litter the River Humber and the surrounding area.

When a vessel for instance lost its sail in a storm or found itself in any trouble, there wasn't a lot that could be done. Distress rockets were carried and in such circumstances fired but the result of these ways of attracting attention were tenuous and they depended on some observant person on another ship or on shore. If such a signal was noticed then the long drawn out routine of finding someone with a boat who would go to the assistance of the ship in distress, certainly, the cameraderie was such that help would be offered and everything possible would be done to help a fellow mariner.

If a vessel ran aground in fog there was no alternative but to sit tight and wait for the next tide and hope that you were out of everybody's way. The next tide would refloat the vessel unless in some circumstances another ship would arrive and try to drag the grounded ship off the bank, but this token of help could often result in the rescuing ship grounding also.

Local fishermen had the knowledge of the tides, currents, and deep water channels, so they knew their way about. It was such men that volunteered their service as crew of the lifeboat. Nothing changed in that way, they were just more co-ordinated and perceptive. Disaster at sea in the Humber area, was, fortunately, rare, but usually a grounding in severe weather would result in the crew taking to the masts if the vessel took a bad list, rockets could be fired and there was an outside chance that someone would see them on shore or other ships in the vicinity.

With the advent of the steam tug in the latter part of the 19th Century, rescue for crew and vessel became more of a possibility, the lasting problem still was communication and the means to attract attention.

In the case of accident or illness at sea, again, help could be very far away, the only hope was a passing ship to which the injured man might be transferred and the hope that the casualty might survive to be treated.

The Humber Estuary has its reputation for north easterly gales which certainly knock the fishing fleet about causing many kinds of difficulties and in some instances the overwhelming force of mountainous waves swept the small vessels to their destruction. In those days compensation paid to the families and dependents of the unfortunate men was very little and such an occurence often resulted in grinding poverty for the families.

Most of the fishing fleet in those days could be described as 'well found', well maintained and able to battle with the elements, but in some cases, old leaky tubs that were risky in the extreme and gave the crew constant problems were sent out by unscrupulous owners whose greed put the unfortunate crew's lives in danger the moment they left port.

Crews were very often under paid and they were very dependent on the generosity of the owners, few of the crews could swim, not much advantage really as exposure in the water did not exactly prolong life, the cork life belts afforded some help but generally you were on your own.

Hard work and long hours was the routine of life aboard the Smacks. The youngest members of the crew would be about 14 and maturity came quickly in those circumstances, the continuous soaking, which was frequent during most days, often resulted in pneumonia or TB, certainly one's physique was put to the test in more than one way; the weaker men either succumbed to the hard life or got out before it was too late, only those who were able to stand the rigours of life at sea in a small boat survived.

The coming of the lifeboat to Cleethorpes did not result in a reduction of mishaps at sea, it was just that the lifeboat could render some added assistance and stand by a ship in trouble, be they big or small and in some cases bring the crews back to port.

In other circumstances, the lifeboat would be required to act as a shepherd to the fishing fleet in bad weather and would stand by to assist the stragglers, who might have been limping home, disabled in some way.

It must be remembered that the early lifeboats manned by local fishermen relied on sheer muscle, OARPOWER, and often in cases of emergency those early craft were sent to perform what would seem today, impossible acts of rescue, which involved placing the lives of these gallant men who sought only to bring their colleagues home safe and sound from a ship in distress, in almost as much danger.

In some situations the lifeboat would be called out to a grounded vessel and on arriving at the scene of the trouble would be asked to 'take an anchor out'. This request meant that the lifeboat would have to go alongside the grounded ship and take the anchor out into deep water and drop it in hoping it would bite on the sea bed then the vessel on the bank would use the purchase to pull the vessel off the bank into deep water. However, lifeboats are not usually regarded as salvage vessels and in many cases the request would be refused, the lifeboat would take the crew off a distressed ship but to place the lifeboat in a hazardous position to refloat a grounded ship would, in many instances, be outside the lifeboats function.

Safety at sea in the latter half of the 19th Century was a matter of fate and good luck. Many fishermen had a fatalistic approach to life at sea, they knew that in the event of mishaps often any assistance would arrive too late or not at all. Such vessels were fishing for sheer survival and a poor quality of life, but slowly improvements and some modernisation of the fishing fleet

gradually emerged. Life on board the small fishing smacks was always austere and hard, the main thought in the Skipper's head was to catch as much fish as possible during the time at sea and the crew worked hard so they had little time to worry about other things. When the weather was bad they battened down everything and waited, if they were still the right way up and on an even keel when the weather moderated fishing would continue. It was certainly no life for the faint hearted, it made men of youths who wanted to learn the ropes and felt they had the sea in their blood and didn't mind getting wet! Lessons were certainly learned and experience gained, the lucky ones survived, the others were either washed overboard by freak waves or walked off the ship before she left port.

Any fishing vessel would go to the assistance of others in distress. A lot of risks were taken to effect assistance, signals by oil lamps were the only way to attract any attention apart from the rockets, it depended on who was watching!

The early lifeboats, being powered by brute force of the crew pulling on the oars, were hard put to tow damaged boats back to port in the appalling weather conditions in which the lifeboats came to be involved. Often it was as much as the lifeboat crew managed to get home themselves, often with many members of crew of a stricken ship.

The reason that Cleethorpes was chosen to have its own Lifeboat Station was due to many factors which fused together and eventually produced results.

It should be realised that the Spurn Lifeboat Station, which was constituted in 1810, only gave a token cover to the local fishing fleets, the area was so large and remote that the Spurn Station could only manage to attend local cases of vessels in distress, and was rather inadequate to be of assistance to the increasing amount of sea borne trade that was consistently using the River Humber and the Estuary.

The main factor that was working in Cleethorpes favour was a charity named the Independent Order of Oddfellows who through their subsidiary, The Manchester Unity Friendly Society, were actually investigating the possibility of donating a lifeboat to the Royal National Lifeboat Institution. However, the Manchester Unity wanted some say in where the lifeboat was to be located. Of course, the most deserving location would benefit.

At their meeting of the Grand Annual Movable Committee held in the Assembly Rooms in Cheltenham on 1st June 1868, the resolution of the sub committee set up to explore the viability of the donation of a lifeboat was discussed at length by the Board of Directors.

With reference to the subscriptions paid to the RNLI, the sum in hand at the time was £520 and it was proposed that this sum be paid over to the RNLI for the provision of a lifeboat. The actual position would be considered after more recommendations had been discussed, a Mr. Burgess had been asked to investigate the best site for the lifeboat and come back with his commendations. He gave his report and findings, he recommended Broadstairs in Kent as a likely place, but after more discussion the Directors required more candidates for the favoured Lifeboat Station, and at their next meeting a Mr. C. S. Ratcliffe suggested that a small seaside community (Cleethorpes on the Lincolnshire Coast) would benefit considerably from having a lifeboat based there. All the Committee were in agreement and the Directors agreed that £620 should be used to construct the Lifeboat Station, and this would allow for the building of the boat and its carriage too. The Directors added that no expense would be spared to obtain the best facilities for the Station.

Meanwhile, following the occurrence of several shipwrecks in the coastal area around Grimsby and Cleethorpes in the early and mid 1860's, a number of Cleethorpes people came together and their spokesman, Mr. Edwin Lloyd, wrote to the RNLI at their HQ in London asking if a lifeboat could be stationed at or near Cleethorpes to ensure some degree of assistance for shipping in distress. There was obviously a need for such a service owing to the rapid growth of the local fishing industry and in the letter Mr. Lloyd mentioned that the Brig 'Saxe Coburg' had been wrecked on Clee Ness Sands 4 days earlier.

Little did Mr. Lloyd know that the wheels of progress were turning slowly and that his letter was having the consideration he thought it deserved.

At a meeting of the RNLI Committee of Management in London on 2nd January 1868, the members of the Committee decided to create a Lifeboat Station at Cleethorpes. Meetings had been held with the Independent Order of Oddfellows and their subsidiary, the Manchester Unity Friendly Society, who were willing to pay for the construction of the actual lifeboat and carriage, also the lifeboat house and other facilities at the resort.

The Manchester Unity Friendly Society already had a branch in Cleethorpes which was established in June 1839 and was named and numbered 1803 'Loyal Fishermen's Rest Lodge' and in the year 1868 they had 100 members who gathered at their hall at the corner of Oole Road, Cleethorpes.

So a new era of hope and potential assistance began to be felt by the crews of the local fishing boats. No doubt the local fishermen would still go to the rescue and aid of their fellows, but ultimately some of the fishermen would volunteer themselves as members of the lifeboat crew, and the thought of a purpose built craft for the express purpose of rescue work had a definite appeal.

In the meantime a 'commodious boathouse' had been built near the Brighton Street Slipway, this area was always known as the 'Fisherman's Slip' so the site was appropriate. The building had been designed by Mr. C. H. Cooke of London, who was the Honorary Architect to the RNLI.

Mr. Lloyd had formed a Committee to support the lifeboat operation and he was delighted at the news that Cleethorpes was to have its own lifeboat soon.

The lifeboat had been constructed by James Woolfe of Shadwell, London and was of the self righting type. She was fitted with self ejecting valves to drain any water shipped into the craft due to severe weather or a total capsize. She was 33ft. long by 8½ft. beam, 12 oars were used for propulsion. The boat had completed here self righting trials in the Regents Canal Dock in London to the eminent admiration of the crowd who had gathered to watch the demonstration. The water shipped during the

ODD FELLOWS' LIFEBOAT;

Launched at CLEETHORPES, August 17th, 1868.

COPYRIGHT.

R. W. WELLS, PHOTO., HULL.

The new Cleethorpes Lifeboat 'Manchester Unity' on show in the old Market Place, Grimsby, prior to ceremonial procession to Cleethorpes and its base.
August 17th, 1868.

capsize had drained away and it was noticed that she had a whale back at each end of the hull for the shelter of rescued passengers. She was the latest type of lifeboat and was voted "A very excellent craft".

To show their gratitude, the Committee of the RNLI presented the 'Manchester Unity Friendly Society' with a copy of thanks inscribed on vellum and a fine model of the lifeboat with a suitable silver tablet and a photography of a lifeboat proceeding to attend a shipwreck. It was later stated by the 'Manchester Unity Friendly Society' that the RNLI had agreed to the new lifeboat being named 'Manchester Unity' in a gesture of thanks and appreciation.

The Directors of the Independent Order of Oddfellows agreed to allow the vessel to be displayed at the Annual Demonstration at the Crystal Palace on 6th August 1868 at the request of the Metropolitan Districts of the aforementioned Order. After the display at the Crystal Palace the lifeboat was taken to Windsor and again put on display for the occasion of Prince Alfred's birthday.

The new lifeboat was taken to Kings Cross and loaded onto a flat wagon with its carriage and equipment and sent to Grimsby where the interested crowds gathered to see it unloaded and eventually placed on display near the Corn Exchange in Grimsby Market Place.

In those early days it was not uncommon for the local lifeboat to be taken to the surrounding Towns for display. In the case of the Cleethorpes lifeboat it is possible that Louth would be visited, it would be a long day out for the Coxswain and crew, all dressed up for the occasion, but the journey would be tiring for the horses that hauled the heavy carriage with the lifeboat proudly carried for all the locals to see. Of course collecting boxes would be shaken under people's noses and some monetary advantage would be gained from the day out.

It was one way that the excellent work of the RNLI could be shown to people who didn't often visit the seaside.

Certainly the arrival of the lifeboat drew a good response among the local population of Grimsby and district and the officials of the RNLI passed among the crowds with their collecting boxes.

Then on Monday August 17th at noon the big moment arrived, all morning the preparations had gone on with all speed and industry.

Finally all was declared ready and the lifeboat on its carriage was hitched up to 6 large horses, all beautifully groomed and polished with shining horse brasses and accroutrements. The procession moved slowly off on its journey to Cleethorpes and the new Lifeboat Station. Brass bands played and many banners were waved, everybody was in a festive mood, the sun shone warmly and the highly polished brass and silver instruments glittered to dazzle. The Oddfellows were well represented by their district delegates from all over the country, their banners being proudly displayed.

In the lifeboat were several local fishermen wearing their cork lifejackets, these fellows were to become some of the lifeboat crew. To strike a melancholy note, also in the boat were 20 orphans, 10 from each of the orphans asylums in Hull under the care of Messrs. Wills and Whittle respectively. These boys displayed bannerets on which was inscribed the name of the vessels in which their fathers sailed in at the time of their deaths.

The lifeboat was preceded by the Grimsby and Lincoln Districts Oddfellows and bringing up the rear were a company of coastguards.

When opposite the Grimsby Town Hall in Town Hall Square, the Hull contingent fell back to allow several private carriages to enter the procession. The first carriage contained the Mayor of Grimsby, Mr. Oates and Mr. J. Fildes (the MP for Grimsby) the Lord Mayor of Kingston upon Hull, (who also enjoyed the Title of Admiral of the Humber) and the Sheriff of Hull, whilst in the second carriage were Messrs. Norwood and Clay, who were local Members of Parliament and Mr. H. Atkinson JP.

As the procession resumed its journey, the houses along the route presented a very colourful picture, being decorated profusely with flags, bunting and evergreens etc. Triumphal arches had been erected and this was a sight to be remembered. On arriving at Cleethorpes sea shore, a great multitude of people awaited the arrival of the procession and a first sight of the lifeboat. It is recorded that the size of the crowd gathered at Cleethorpes that day exceeded 50,000 people, never again would the little seaside resort see such a mighty gathering of people.

The decorations and general appearance of the resort was to be seen to be believed, the atmosphere was one of a carnival and a day of joy, people had come to Cleethorpes from miles around and they were going to enjoy their day out.

The procession slowly wound itself down the high cliff to Brighton Street, the Boathouse and the cobbled slipway, the excited crowds jostling and pushing to get a good view of the scene.

The boat on its carriage was eased down the slipway and the horses unhitched. The regular crew climbed into the lifeboat wearing their oilskins, frocks and sou'westers and posed for photographs. Then the naming of the lifeboat ceremony was carried out by Miss Walker, who was the daughter of the Grand Master of the Oddfellows. She named the vessel 'Manchester Unity', the hurrahs and cheers rang out and tumultuous applause broke out, the boat was then coupled up to the waiting horses again and pulled out to the water's edge some 300 yards distant and after about 20 minutes the boat was pulled off the carriage and floated clear, a demonstration of the boat's abilities was performed including a capsize, much to the admiration of the onlooking crowds.

At 7p.m. a Banquet was attended by the distinguished guests and other visiting dignatories in a Marquee erected on the green shore.

The Mayor of Grimsby, Coun Oates, presided at this occasion and various loyal toasts were proposed and responded to, the Members of Parliament refrained from any political allusions.

A balcony or viewing platform had been erected at the break of the High Cliff to afford the distinguished guests a good view of the proceedings. This facility was soon occupied by these fortunate people and their friends in spite of misgivings for their safety as the structure didn't look too safe, these fears were proved correct when at the close of the speeches, part of the platform on the land side

gave way. There were sounds of distress uttered by the ladies both on and off the structure, but luckily no one was hurt, but had the other end on the water side collapsed, more serious consequences might have occurred as many people on the balcony might have been tipped down the Cliff with disastrous results!!!

So ended Cleethorpe's big day, a day to be recorded as the largest gathering of all time in the resort, 50,000 people in the Town even these days would be frowned on by the local Authorities, but in those far off days the coming of the lifeboat was a moment not to be missed and such an occasion, which would not have been hyped in any way, would have been advertised by word of mouth.

There is no doubt that Cleethorpes had pulled off a triumphal attraction and the Lifeboat Station became a visitors place of interest, and the latter part of the 19th Century brought many thousands of people wanting to see the sea and sniff the beneficial ozone for its health-giving properties!!!

However, let us not forget the difficulties experienced by the crew of the 'Manchester Unity' as on winter's nights they grappled with the problems of catching the horses that were so necessary to haul the lifeboat and carriage down the beach to the often far off tide. Knowing a little about horses I can imagine the difficulties the crew met with, a recalcitrant horse is big trouble and they have a mind of their own, normally horses like water but not up to their necks as could often be the case. Once in the water they would be ridden by their handlers, coupled up to the heavy and unwieldly carriage, maybe bogged down by this time in soft clinging mud, no wonder that two of these gallant animals were drowned in particularly dreadful weather conditions. As happened on some occasions, the lifeboat would be floated off its carriage only to be flung bodily back onto the beach by the next gigantic wave, then the whole routine would have to be started all over again now with tiring men and weary horses, big as they were. Meanwhile the ship in distress was waiting hopefully that help was on the way, it was . . . . . .

The first meeting of the local committee of the RNLI formed to support the recently installed lifeboat at Cleethorpes was held at the Royal Hotel, Cleethorpes

Road, Grimsby on 3rd April 1869. In the Chair was Capt. J. W. Grant Thorold, also present was the Mayor of Grimsby, Mr. T. Oates, Mr. E. Bannister, the Rev. Trebcock, the Rev. D. Jones, and the Honorary Secretary.

Satisfaction was expressed with the arrangements for the inauguration and dedication, in every way a celebration to remember, of the lifeboat 'Manchester Unity', which was housed in a splendid 'commodius' boathouse near the Brighton street slipway designed by Mr. C. H. Cooke, the RNLI Architect, and ably constructed by the local building firm of Nollingham and Condor at a cost of £227.

Highlights of the momentous occasion were remembered with pleasure and the Chairman was happy to allow the reminiscences to go unchecked for a while, the event certainly had made history, never before had so many people crammed themselves into Cleethorpes, records mention crowds of around 50,000 souls. The Annual Regatta had always been popular but the arrival of the lifeboat had broken all bounds in general rejoicing and spectacle.

It was noted that the compliance of Sidney Sussex College of Cambridge in their co-operation in allowing the lease of land near Brighton Street for the construction of the lifeboat house, it was agreed that thanks to be recorded in the minutes to these good people. Also mentioned was the great help and support of the Independent Order of Oddfellows and their local subsidiary charity, the Manchester Unity Friendly Society, whose gift and overwhelming co-operation made the Lifeboat and its station possible, thanks to the above were also recorded in the minutes.

Capt. Ward, RN, Inspector of Lifeboats, who had been closely involved with the lifeboat and the station from the start, observed that a hardstanding or chalkway be constructed in front of the boathouse and that tenders had been sent out and advertised in the local Press, only one tender had been received from a local builder named Brown and his estimate of £52 was accepted.

The London Committee of the RNLI presented the Cleethorpes RNLI station with a handsome barometer for the use of the fishermen of Cleethorpes and a 'substantial brick pillar' was erected in front of Chapman's Hotel near the Lifeboat house, the cost of the brick pillar was £4-2-0d.

The Cleethorpes and Grimsby branch of the RNLI finances were fairly healthy as they showed a balance of £40-6-11d and a letter from the branch was sent to the London Committee to this effect.

A copy of the Lifeboat Journal had been received and it was agreed that each member of the committee should pay for a copy of the Journal and that it should be available to the general public.

A letter was read out by the Secretary from the London Committee thanking the local branch for the sum of £20 which had been sent to London.

Letters from Goole had been received regarding Messrs. Tupman and Lewis concerning life salvage claims invoked by these two men. The Chairman remarked that this matter was in no way connected with the RNLI and the men concerned should be told to deal with their own salvage claims and not to have them addressed to the RNLI!

Mention was also made about the excellent conduct of the lifeboat crew on the occasion of the recent heavy gales and appalling weather in which the boat had been launched to go on exercise, in fact the lifeboat was not to be called out to a distress call for over two years after her installation at Cleethorpes. She certainly was taken out on regular exercise to allow the crew to familiarise themselves with the boat's handling and manoeuvrability and to this extent the crew worked well and efficiently.

On the occasion of the 3rd committee meeting held on 3rd January 1870 at the Royal Hotel, it was learnt that the crew had held a meeting and after much deliberation had elected a Coxswain, Mr. Sam Stephenson. The Order of Oddfellows always had a representative on the Committee and at this meeting Mr. P. K. Seddon was appointed.

Some discussion ensued concerning the removal of the lifeboat from Cleethorpes to Grimsby, apparently the Manchester, Sheffield and Lincolnshire Railway Company had offered a berth in the Royal Dock Basin but it was to be another 12 years before this offer was taken up.

Meanwhile the 'Manchester Unity' was used to exercise and admired by onlookers, who, when the weather permitted, lined the shore to see the boat go through the manoeuvres and exercises. Capt. Ward was well satisfied with the boat's performance and the crews attitude to the job.

The first rescue service performed by the 'Manchester Unity' was on August 29th 1870, when the lifeboat answered a call to assist two vessels in difficulties in heavy seas and a north westerly gale. She first went to the aid of a Dutch fishing smack, 'Jan Wilhelmina' of NIEU DIEP, which had gone aground at Tetney Haven, after much difficulty manoeuvering to get alongside the vessel she finally managed to get into position and took the 2 man crew off and then rowed to the second vessel in trouble. She was the Brig 'Hope' of Jersey and she too had run aground at Grainthorpe Haven. Her crew had done their best but they were unable to prevent the vessel from moving further and further onto the sand bank. The 'Manchester Unity' went alongside and transferred the crew of 9 to the lifeboat and set off back to Cleethorpes, arriving there after 10 hours at sea.

On November 10th 1872, the 'Manchester Unity' was launched to go to the assistance of the sloop 'Queen Victoria' of Kings Lynn which had gone aground on the infamous sand banks off Grainthorpe Haven in the midst of a north easterly gale. In truly deplorable weather and heavy seas, the lifeboat managed to get alongside the sloop and rescue 2 men, they then set off for Cleethorpes having a terrible time and sustaining a tremendous buffeting from the mountainous seas. The gallant crew emphasising the courage and selfless dedication to duty so necessary to men who manned the Lifeboats.

Meanwhile, in January 1873, the local RNLI committee received a letter from the London committee of management complaining that they hadn't heard from the Cleethorpes local committee, no explanation was given for this lack of communication.

It was common place in those days for a neighbouring lifeboat to call for assistance from another lifeboat, and an example is given when on December 9th 1874 the Cleethorpes lifeboat and the Donna Nook boat went to the aid of the schooner 'Kathleen' of Kings Lynn bound from Rochester in Kent to Goole. The N.N.E. gale force winds had whipped up heavy seas, the 'Kathleen' had dropped anchor to ride out the storm but she was very close to the notorious North Haile sand bank that had claimed so many ill-fated vessels in the past. Conditions became so bad that the vessel dragged her anchor and rode up the sand bank and as the weather worsened, the crew, who had been battling with the elements and had been knocked about to exhaustion, had to cut away the rigging. Meanwhile the Donna Nook lifeboat 'North Briton' on her carriage was hauled along the foreshore by 6 heavy horses to try to find a place to launch the boat from the carriage. At about 9am the crew and helpers attempted to launch the 'North Briton' but as soon as she left the carriage, the heavy seas swept her back on the beach. After about half an hour they tried again and this time, the lifeboat got away to meet the Cleethorpes boat that was also being thrown around by the heavy seas. Together they reached the stricken schooner and gave assistance, between them they took the crew off and the 'Manchester Unity' managed to get a line aboard the 'Kathleen' and the long, slow, tow into safe waters began. Imagine the 12 men heaving on the oars, the lifeboat being swept from wave to wave, the tow slackening, then being drawn bar tight, the crew of the 'Kathleen' huddled in the whale backs, frightened and shivering, the stoutly built lifeboat creaking under the tremendous strain of hauling the wreck through the wind blown seas. At about 3pm, land was sighted and the 'Manchester Unity' beached near her slip, the horses were waiting with the carriage, the wind had dropped somewhat but the rain still poured down. The helpers soon had the boat on the carriage and the survivors were taken care of by the sympathetic fishermen. The 'Kathleen' was beached, she could wait until the next favourable opportunity to patch her up and take her to Grimsby for repair.

This rescue service illustrated the co-operation and help that one lifeboat would give another, the RNLI was there to render assistance to all, and the service worked together.

On November 20th 1875, distress signals were seen

from Cleethorpes indicating a ship in distress. The lifeboat was launched at 4.30pm, in the dusk conditions the 'Manchester Unity' rowed out to find a Danish schooner, the 'Fortuna', had lost an anchor in the heavy seas and gale force winds, some of her gear and sail had been swept overboard leaving her helpless and at the mercy of the waves. Her crew were by now totally exhausted and her Master asked the lifeboat to come alongside and some of the lifeboat crew to come aboard and help to man the salvage pumps. After some difficulty this was possible and the day was saved by the appearance of a steam tug which took the Schooner in tow and she was taken into Grimsby Docks.

At the 8th Meeting of the local RNLI committee on February 22nd 1876, it was agreed to invite the Countess of Yarborough to accept the position of President in place of her late husband. It was also resolved to ask the Collector of Customs if the collecting bowl could be placed in the shipping office at the Customs House.

Later we are told that Lady Yarborough had agreed to accept the position of President of the Branch.

It was also reported that the lifeboat had been launched to go to the assistance of the schooner 'Ninian', which had been driven aground on a shoal off Thrunscoe.

The question of the hard standing in front of the lifeboat house again raised its ugly head, the heavy seas were pounding it to pieces and the recommendation was to repair it again. Capt. Ward had studied the position so closely and he came up with 3 recommendations; 1, to pull the lifeboat house down and re-position it further inland. 2, to repair the hard standing again as permanent as possible in its present position. 3, to remove the lifeboat altogether and re-locate it in the Royal Dock Basin at Grimsby. The question was asked of the Secretary as to how much it would cost to hire a steam tug to tow the lifeboat out of the Dock Basin. After much discussion it was resolved to ask for estimates for the repair of the hard standing and it is further recorded in the minutes that the cost of this work was £105-19-0d in 1877.

At a Meeting of the local committee on 15th April 1878 held at the Royal Hotel, Grimsby, a deputation from the Manchester Unity Friendly Society was received to voice their concern about alleged dilatory practices indulged by the lifeboat crew who failed to reach the vessel 'Antias' of Goole and the crew of 5 men had been lost. The Chairman hastened to re-assure the leader of the deputation that no charge of negligence should be attached to the lifeboat crew who had to take 3 volunteers in place of 3 crewmen who were unable to answer the call out. The lifeboat had been properly launched and had cruised around the area of the position of the 'Antias' to no avail, a case of willingness to help and assist but on this occasion, too late. It was agreed to send a statement to the local Press for their publication. The 'Manchester Unity' was launched to go to the aid of the 'Mathilde' of Laurent on October 8th 1878, the weather was appalling and the difficulties experienced in launching the boat in such extreme conditions was to cause the deaths by drowning of two of the heavy horses that hauled the lifeboat and its carriage to the water's edge for the movement of the carriage into the sea.

A very sad occasion, the horses were so essential for this purpose and to see the poor animals struggle out of their depth attempting to find solid ground for their large hooves was harrowing. It was a wonder that the horses were not lost before if one considers the extremes of weathers they were expected to drag the carriage and boat to the water line which in some cases was a long way, the tide goes a long way out on the East Coast. On this occasion the RNLI paid the owner of the horses £50 compensation.

Needless to say the launch was not successful and the matter was discussed at the local meeting of the RNLI held on 16th November 1878 at Mr. Bannister's Office on the Fish Docks, Grimsby. It was agreed to pay the drivers of the horses 2/6d extra on account of their exertions and for the long time they had spent in the swirling water trying to free the other horses. It was also agreed that for night launches the drivers should receive 3/6d instead of 2/6d.

It was also reported that the lifeboat had been out on service in the afternoon of November 15th (the day preceding the committee meeting) when distress rockets were seen coming from a vessel which seemed to be lying off Tetney Haven. The 'Manchester Unity' was rowed out in a terrible northerly gale and very heavy seas, the vessel in trouble turned out to be the brigantine 'Sea Flower' of Seaham and she had grounded off Grainthorpe. The skill and expertise of the lifeboat crew was put to the test to get alongside, but finally the lifeboat managed to manoeuvre alongside but in so doing sustained some damage to the boat and several oars were broken such was the violence of the seas. Fortunately the crew of 5 from the 'Sea Flower' were transferred to the 'Manchester Unity' and taken back to Cleethorpes and safety.

The local committee were also told of the gallantry of the crew of the shoreboat 'Deerhound' when they went to the aid of the 'Eliza' of Ipswich after she ran aground off Clee Ness. The 'Deerhound' took the crew of 4 off the stranded vessel and brought them back to safety.

The severe storm on May 2nd 1879 damaged the hardstanding in front of the lifeboat house and also undermined the building's foundations. Discussions again took place about the possibility of moving the whole lifeboat operation to Grimsby's Royal Dock Basin and a site inspection by Capt. Ward and some senior members of the RNLI had approved the MS&L's preferred site. Meanwhile, repairs to the hardstanding and foundations of the lifeboat house had been put in order at a cost of £130-15-0.

At the meeting of the local RNLI committee held at Mr. E. Bannister's office on 24th September 1880, it was agreed to ask the local Clergy if they would have an annual silver collection for the RNLI. The Coxswain was present at this meeting and he gave his account of the delay in launching the lifeboat during the recent appalling weather.The committee, having listened carefully to the explanation, expressed their confidence in the Coxswain and crew. The Coxswain also mentioned the difficulties in assembling a crew in bad weather.

Captain St. Vincent Nepean (who was a Senior Official from the London Committee and was visiting the area) was requested to consult Captain Jewitt (The Dockmaster at Grimsby) to enquire whether a dependable crew would be available during periods of bad weather if the lifeboat was moved to Grimsby.

At the Meeting held at Mr. Bannister's Office on February 3rd 1881, reference was made to the fact that the lifeboat had not been out on practice, the explanation given was the hardstanding in front of the lifeboat house was breaking up again due to the heavy seas breaking over it. Its condition had deteriorated so badly that the lifeboat could not be moved safely without causing damage to the lifeboat and its carriage. Some discussion then ensued about the usual possibility of moving the whole operation to Grimsby.

At the next meeting at the usual venue, a report from Capt. Ward, the District RNLI Inspector, was read out and the relevant facts were as follows:-

The situation at Cleethorpes as regards the lifeboat station had been deteriorating so badly that Captain Ward recommended that the whole operation should be moved to Grimsby, mainly because of the flat nature of the beach and the lifeboat could not be launched without risk or delay, also the foundations and hardstanding in front of the lifeboat house presented continuous problems and were always requiring maintenance work. In view of these problems and the RNLI's concern with speedy turn out and efficient routines, Capt. Ward felt that there was now no point in prolonging the operation of the RNLI station at Cleethorpes.

The Chairman, therefore, was asked to accept the Manchester, Sheffield and Lincolnshire Railway Companies offer and move to the Royal Dock Basin in Grimsby. The Chairman was also to ask if a boathouse and slipway could be constructed to house the lifeboat at its new site. The committee having inspected the new location and expressed their approval, it was agreed to ask if the barometer could be moved from its pillar and placed in a suitable position near the entrance to the Royal Dock. It was also resolved as a matter of courtesy to inform the HM coastguard as to the removal of the lifeboat and the lifeboat station facility and transfer the operation to the Royal Dock Basin at Grimsby, also informed was Capt. Jewitt, the Dock Master, who was to be informed by telegraph when the lifeboat was to be launched. He would then set the machinery into motion.

Discussion then moved to recommend the erection of a stout fence to protect the Cleethorpes Lifeboat Station from 'rough people' who might vandalise the property.

So Cleethorpes and her lifeboat were to part company. The lifeboat had performed sterling service during its time at the resort, and had gained many friends. The 'Manchester Unity' had been launched 15 times on service and had saved 23 lives. Cleethorpes had changed considerably during those 14 years, the resort had grown and had developed both socially and commercially. Grimsby had become the premier fishing port and success was evident in the prosperity to be seen everywhere, but eras have to end and Cleethorpes had to lose a tourist and tripper attraction, no longer would the children ask to see the lifeboat at Cleethorpes.

However, the 'Manchester Unity' was to remain in service for another 5 years at her new home in Grimsby.

All that remained of the erstwhile lifeboat scene at Cleethorpes was the fenced off lifeboat house and the crumbling hardstanding being slowly eroded by the waves. Luckily, the signs of decay and abandonment were not allowed to become too desolate as the boathouse was demolished after a short while and all signs of a lifeboat station disappeared.

When, in January 1882, the erstwhile Cleethorpes Lifeboat Station and lifeboat were moved en bloc to the Royal Dock Basin in Grimsby, Cleethorpes had developed considerably during the 14 years that the lifeboat was based at the resort. The main reason for the development and prosperity was the coming of the Railway in 1863. The MS&L Railway Company had long foreseen the potential in Cleethorpes and had waited for the right moment to push the line from Grimsby the few miles to Cleethorpes. The Railway Company had bought up various parcels and areas of land in the resort and saw the value in so doing. The Railway connection brought much needed trade and with it prosperity for all. The building of the Pier gave Cleethorpes an attraction and as befits a holiday resort such development was necessary and gave work to local industry. Cleethorpes Railway Station couldn't be nearer the beach and a passenger could literally get out of the train onto the sands!

The Lifeboat Station had been an attraction for the visitor, who came from the West and South Yorkshire towns and the Midlands areas, such was the wide publicity that the up and coming seaside resort attracted. Children especially were fascinated by the lifeboat and wanted to know all about it, usually there would be one of the crew in attendance to explain the working and activities of the lifeboat and its station. Visitors were reminded that the collecting box placed in a prominent position was so necessary for the continued use of the boat and station. The boat, looking so business like in the boathouse, seemed so substantial and re-assuring to the visitor with its 12 oars no doubt operated by 12 muscular men!

Cleethorpes had rapidly become a place to visit on the Lincolnshire Coast and many who hadn't seen the German Ocean and who were believing the tales of theraputic benefits could be derived from sniffing the ozone would take a train ride from Rotherham for what seems a paltry 6/- return. From Nottingham the return fare was only 5/- so Cleethorpes was accessible from the South, West and East Yorkshire and the Midlands, in addition to rail facilities many people travelled on the steam packets from Hull.

The annual tea party of the Primitive Methodists attracted a large number of visitors. Trips were run from all parts of the Midlands for the faithful to indulge themselves in tea cakes and religion and have a good look around Cleethorpes at the same time, a dual purpose and perhaps the soul was refreshed by the tea and the ozone!

The local transport between the two towns of Grimsby and Cleethorpes was the track made by horse drawn wagonettes, horse drawn omnibuses or shanks pony. Certainly in those far off days people were more active and durable, they would think nothing of walking 7 or 8 miles per day and the children were encouraged to be independent and if they couldn't afford the bus fare, they walked.

Grimsby welcomed the Lifeboat Station and the crew, the date was January 1882 and a new era was beginning. Levi Stephenson had retired as Cox and it was recorded in the minutes the appreciation of his sterling work and dedication to the job as Coxswain of the Cleethorpes lifeboat.

Mr. F. Dawson of Victoria Chambers stayed on as Hon. Secretary, the rest of the committee stayed in Office.

A boathouse had been built with a slipway on the north west side of the tidal Royal Dock Basin at a cost of £576 and the lifeboat was on a carriage for launching.

The following signals were agreed for assembling the crew to launch the lifeboat:-

By day, sound rockets and fly the flag.

By night, sound red rockets.

At the local RNLI committee meeting held at Mr. Bannister's office on January 13th, it was reported that the 'Manchester Unity' had been called out for the first time from Grimsby on December 6th 1882 when distress rockets were seen coming from a ship later identified as the 'Fiona' of Glasgow which seemed in difficulties in the east south east gale. On reaching the vessel however, assistance was refused and the lifeboat rowed back to Grimsby somewhat annoyed. A few hours later the schooner 'Laura Ann' of Faversham had dropped anchor in a dangerous position at the mouth of the river. The 'Manchester Unity' pulled alongside and some of the lifeboat's crew boarded the 'Laura Ann' and helped her crew to raise the anchor, the schooner was then taken in tow back to Grimsby by a tug. Mr. G. Grant had been appointed Coxswain in place of Levi Stephenson but his tenure of the position was short for the unfortunate man was washed overboard the lifeboat and drowned early in June 1883. Tribute to this brave man was paid by the Chairman of the RNLI committee, Mr. E. Bannister. Joshua Hudson of 30 Watkin Street, Grimsby, who had been a promising crew member was appointed Coxswain in his place.

The problem of sand being washed onto the slipway was seen as an obstruction and troublesome and Capt. Jewitt was authorised to engage a fellow to keep the slipway clear at all times, a sum of £10 was set aside for this purpose.

The District Inspector had inspected the Station and Lifeboat and expressed his satisfaction.

The lifeboat was launched at 2.30 p.m. on March 6th 1883 to go to the assistance of the schooner 'Mary Coad' of Port Isaac bound from Antwerp to Middlesborough which was seen to be flying distress signals while at anchor in the river about $\frac{1}{2}$ mile west of the Bull buoy. The lifeboat when alongside and 3 of the crew went aboard the 'Mary Coad', they found the Captain and crew totally exhausted, the steering gear had failed and it was feared that they might run aground. After a while a tug arrived and a tow line was secured with the intention being to tow the schooner to Grimsby, but after a short while the tow line parted and difficulties were experienced in getting aboard the 'Mary Coad' to attach other lines. This problem, however, was overcome and 2 tow lines were secured and the tow recommended, this time all went well and the vessel was brought into Grimsby without further trouble.

The Grimsby lifeboat was called to assist the schooner 'Margaret' of Caernarvon on December 12th 1883. This ship had run aground on the Trinity Sands, the weather was bad and a full gale was blowing from the north. The lifeboat managed to reach the schooner and rescue the crew but the 'Margaret' had to be abandoned as she was now in a very derelict condition and her hull was too badly damaged, also the seas had started to break her up. The crew of 4 were taken back to Grimsby.

A Telegram received at 9.45 a.m. on February 28th 1884 at Grimsby requested the services of the lifeboat to attend the brig 'R. W. Parry' of Blyth, this vessel was eventually found aground off Grainthorpe. As the 'Manchester Unity' approached her it was obvious that she was in a parlous condition, the seas were breaking over her decks. With great difficulty the lifeboat managed to get near the wreck when a gigantic wave threw her onto the 'R. W. Parry', causing considerable damage and breaking three oars. Fortunately the lifeboat survived the event and managed to pull clear as the 8 men crew of the wreck were dragged into the lifeboat, which then began a slow exhausting way home. Luckily, a Grimsby tug appeared by chance and took the battered lifeboat in tow.

Shortly after this rescue, the Coxswain resigned. He (Mr. Hudson) felt that he could no longer give the time or application to this demanding job, so a Mr. John Brown was appointed in his place.

At a Meeting of the local committee of the RNLI held in Mr. Bannister's office on May 19th 1886, the committee was addressed by Captain the Hon. H. W. Chetwynd, RNLI Inspector of Lifeboats, this gentleman came to discuss the possibility of stationing a larger lifeboat at Grimsby as the present boat was out of date and wanting extensive renovations.

Grimsby was indeed lucky because on October 7th 1887 a new lifeboat arrived at Grimsby. She was 38ft long with a 9ft beam, self righting and she had been built by Forrests of Limehouse London at the cost of £624 and she was the gift of the Independent Order of Oddfellows and their subsidiary the Manchester Unity Friendly Society, and like the previous boat, the name 'Manchester Unity' was carried on this new Lifeboat.

Some minor modifications to the slipway at the Royal Dock Basin at Grimsby were necessary. The old lifeboat was taken into the RNLI reserve pool. The new boat performed well and her crew liked her, she was called out to the assistance of the Smack 'Gladstone' of Grimsby, but when the lifeboat approached the Smack she was waved away refusing assistance. However, the lifeboat crew were given £15 for their efforts on a wasted call out.

Grimsby was pleased that the lifeboat was now stationed in the Dock Basin, it gave some assurance to Mariners that potential help could be called on in emergency conditions. Visitors were encouraged to visit the Lifeboat House and view the lifeboat and equipment, there always were questions for the visitor to ask and a collecting box to pour coppers into.

The local committee too, promoted the cause enthusiastically and raised considerable sums of money, retaining some but the main amount went to the London committee. Collecting boxes were placed at strategic locations all over the Fish and Commercial Docks, the facilities were very profitable. Flag days were held at regular intervals in the two Towns, usually on market days and again the ladies who wielded the boxes were well supported, the local committee was very active and was very good at delegating responsibilities, something

of a 'social somewhat elitist cameraderie' being the description given to the committee by some outsiders.

The new lifeboat was called to the aid of the barque 'Milford' of Newcastle (which was the only effective rescue carried out by this lifeboat), this took place on February 3rd 1889.

The 'Milford' was bound for her home port from Goole in ballast, in the severe north easterly gale and mountainous seas she ran aground $1\frac{1}{2}$ miles up the River from Grimsby. Her crew signalled for help by firing rockets, but as the 'Manchester Unity' approached the stricken vessel she too ran aground and on the falling tide remained stuck until the next morning. She then refloated and completed her assistance to the barque taking off the Master and his son, the rest of her crew remained on board until a tug arrived and towed the vessel into Grimsby.

As a result of a telegram from a Mr. Houlden of South Somercotes, the 'Manchester Unity' was called out to find a large vessel that this gentleman had seen in difficulties aground on the Haile Sand. After a considerable time searching the area in question, the lifeboat could not find the vessel in distress. It was thought that she may have gone down or floated and continued her journey. However, the lifeboat had acted in good faith and had attempted to effect an assistance.

The Coxswain was of the opinion that the lifeboat needed a crew of 15 and not 12, which would make a difference of £3 in additional payments.

At a committee meeting held at the Bannister Office on 13th January 1891, it was reported that the slipway had been damaged as a result of a collision involving the 'SS Marianna' and £9 worth of damaged had been caused. This sum had been paid for by the Ship's Master, Captain Hansen.

In the early Summer of 1891 Mr. C. R. Barr was appointed Coxswain in place of John Brown, the 2nd Coxswain being forced to retire because of ill health.

Not every member of the crew could stand the rigours and sheer hard work necessary to propel the heavy and unwieldly boat, and it was beyond the physical capabilities of some of the crew who invariably soon realised

Grimsby Lifeboat "Manchester Unity".
1894 - 1904

their limitations and dropped out making way for men stronger and fitter in wind and limb to endure the strength sapping duties of rowing mile after mile in a heavy oilskin 'Frock', heavy sea boots and many layers of woollen clothing underneath to keep out the Winter's chill. One can imagine the sweat and discomfort endured by these brave men who obviously put their own safety on the line when going out to rescue others, their own families must have worried about the dangers their loved ones were going through trying to find a ship in distress on a dark Winter's night.

On October 14th 1892, the 'Manchester Unity' was launched to go to the assistance of a vessel in distress off South Somercotes. A telegram had been received from the observant Mr. Houlden who had raised the alarm. The lifeboat searched the area without success but found no trace of a vessel, it was later learned that the ship had broken up and that her crew had taken to the boat and had reached the shore safely, the cargo of deals carried by the ship had washed ashore.

Tragedy struck the Lifeboat Station on November 18th 1893, the lifeboat was launched at 5.30 pm in a full gale and tremendous seas to go to the aid of a steamer that was reported aground near Donna Nook (One wonders why the Donna Nook boat did not or could not go to this vessel?). However, a dredger and several lighters were blocking the entrance to the Royal Dock Basin and in the struggle to get the lifeboat on its way to the distress call, the Coxswain Mr. Barr was thrown overboard and before his colleagues could pull him back on board he was crushed between the lifeboat and the jetty. In spite of the attempts to revive him and all the desperate care, Mr. Barr died of his injuries. A local fund was set up to raise money to help his family and dependants, the RNLI gave £250 to set the fund going in appreciation of his services.

The 'Manchester Unity' had been badly damaged by the heavy seas and gale force winds that fatal night. She had been thrown against the supports of the jetty and the stout wooden piles, so bad was the damage that she was taken back to London and the RNLI's Storeyard for examination and an assessment of her future use.

A relief lifeboat was immediately sent to Grimsby by rail, she was a 38ft by 9ft beam self righter and she was known as 'Reserve No.3' and she had been built by Livie Bros. in 1890.

Some time elapsed before news of the examination of the Grimsby Lifeboat was received in Grimsby, the news was bad, the lifeboat had been damaged beyond economical repair.

The new Coxswain, Robert Tye, and the crew liked the relief lifeboat and it was decided that she could stay as the Grimsby Lifeboat and that she should take the name 'Manchester Unity'. The Oddfellows agreed.

Mr. Campion was appointed 2nd Coxswain shortly after, the Chairman of the local branch RNLI committee, Mr. E. Bannister, informed Mrs. Barr that she would be looked after as £300 had been deposited in a bank account at Lincoln allowing her £3 per month! She already owned a shrimp boat that was in need of repair and some money was given to her for this purpose.

At the Meeting held at Mr. Bannister's office of the local committee on December 13th 1894, it was revealed that some person had written to Mr. Bannister stating that there was STILL a need for a lifeboat at Cleethorpes.

Mr. Oates was appointed as Collector of Subscriptions as Captain Maltby yearned for a quiet life!

It was reported that the lifeboat had been out on practice on four occasions during the first year of service in Grimsby, satisfaction was expressed by Capt. Holmes, the local Lifeboat Inspector. However, he had reservations about several members of the crew who had been seen worse for drink with the 2nd Coxswain H. Charlton. The crewmen involved were Crosby and Jones, these people had been severely admonished and warned to their future conduct.

A committee member, Mr. Williams, suggested that on the next occasion the boat went out on exercise why not go to Cleethorpes and give a demonstration of the craft's abilities then have some of the crew go onto the Pier with the collecting boxes? It was agreed that this should be done.

At a Committee Meeting of the local branch held in Mr. Bannister's office on May 7th 1897, the discussion mainly concerned the possibility of Grimsby having a steam lifeboat, Captain Holmes had the details, she would be 56 ft long by 14ft beam and displacement of 32 tons, she was propellor driven, unlike her sister ships that are pressure jet driven. This class of experimental lifeboats had been built for evaluation, only 6 of them had been constructed by J. S. White of Cowes, Isle of Wight. Modest success had been achieved and the RNLI was anxious to try one out at Grimsby. Grimsby was to have the 'James Stevens No.3' which was powered by a single 180hp compound steam engine and on trials she had attained $8^1/_2$ knots. It was said that steam could be raised in 25 minutes but the locals doubted this claim, she would require 2 permanent engineers and two firemen.

Meanwhile the conventional boat was launched to go to the aid of several vessels in distress on January 28th 1897. The vessels concerned were in difficulties in the Tetney area. A telegram from the Coastguard at Donna Nook asked for assistance, (one again wonders where the Donna Nook boat was? perhaps it was already out on call, hence the need for the Grimsby boat.) Great difficulty was experienced getting the Lifeboat out of the Dock Basin owing to high seas and driving winds, no tugs were available and it was not until 3.30am, (some 3 hours later) when the 'Manchester Unity' was able to get into the river and proceed to the rescue. When she arrived in the Tetney area, three vessels were seen to aground on the beach; they were the schooner 'Union' of Portsmouth and Nos 41 and 42 which were coal laden lighters belonging to Cory Bros of London. After standing by for a while it was clear that the lifeboat could not do anything to help as the crews had been taken off. She then rowed back to Grimsby.

Questions were raised by Captain Holmes at a committee meeting of the RNLI held on March 25th 1898 held at Mr. Bannister's office. The serious nature of Captain Holmes's questions concerned the performance of the lifeboat as to 'Why did it take 1 hour 25 minutes to get the crew together?'. One wonders if it was necessary to go round the pubs looking for members of the crew? Apparently the lifeboat had been called out to the assistance of a ship in distress, signal or distress rockets had been seen by vigilant observers and the Grimsby Lifeboat House had been alerted. When the crew had been assembled the 'Manchester Unity' was launched and proceeded to the vicinity of the distress rockets. The lifeboat searched the area but was unable to find the ship which was the 'Harebell' of Sunderland and she was in ballast and she had run aground. A sea mist enveloped the area and inspite of attempts to find the grounded vessel, no sign of the 'Harebell' was seen. After about 3 hours the Coxswain decided to return to Grimsby.

In retrospect, it is difficult to take issue with the actions of the Coxswain. The difficulty in assembling the crew was admitted to be unacceptable but this was the first time such delay had happened and steps would be taken to prevent any further delays in future.

Captain Holmes cross examined Robert Tye, and the crew. It was obvious that Holmes had made his mind up about the episode, also he had decided to get rid of Tye at all costs. Holmes accused Tye of 'Lack of Judgement and Pluck,' he also accused Tye of not even trying to find the 'HAREBELL'. Where he obtained the information that the 'HAREBELL' was only 2-300 yards away from the lifeboat is certainly obscure and not credible, to make things even more bizarre it appeared that the crew of the 'HAREBELL' rowed themselves ashore and were picked up by a man with a horse and cart.

For his negligence and complete lack of judgement, the Coxswain, Robert Tye, was asked to resign, and the crew would be completely re-organised by the Hon. Secretary. On September 13th 1897, the following information was published in Grimsby News concerning the provision of a steam lifeboat for Grimsby's RNLI Station, the details are as follows:-

'Considerable satisfaction will be felt amongst the maritime community at the announcement that it is the intention of the Royal National Lifeboat Institution to place a steam lifeboat at Grimsby. This vessel to be one of two about to be constructed, the other going to Padstow in Cornwall.

Cleethorpes was made a Lifeboat Station 29 years ago, but owing to difficulties of launching and manning, the lifeboat from there was removed to Grimsby in 1882 and afterwards was superseded by the present fine craft.

Both boats have a noble record of life and property saving. As is known, the steam lifeboat is quite an innovation, there being as yet only three afloat in the United Kingdom, the last being the 'Queen' which was launched on the Thames last week, and is to be stationed at New Brighton for service in the Port of Liverpool. This class of vessel, which is of about thirty tons displacement, are sub-divided by steel bulkheads into many watertight compartments, the propelling power is hydraulic, the system being that of forcing the sea water through fore and aft outputs.

The need for a steam lifeboat at Grimsby will be understood when it is remembered that the Lifeboat Station is some seven miles from the mouth of the Humber, and that as the dangerous gales on the Coast are nearly always from the north east, neither oars nor sails are of much value as a means of propulsion under such circumstances. The services of a steam tug to tow the lifeboat have generally to be engaged, whereas a steam lifeboat would reach the river mouth from Grimsby by her own power in about an hour. The matter has been informally considered by the local committees, although nothing was decided. An Inspector of the Institution, however, visited Grimsby last May and talked the matter over with Captain Jewitt who expressed the opinion that such a vessel would be of considerable service at Grimsby, Captain Jewitt, however, has, we believe, received no official intimation upon the subject. It may be pointed out that nearly the whole of the other eastern lifeboat stations are upon the sea coast and that therefore the necessity for steam power does not exist to the same extent as at Grimsby'.

The steam lifeboat 'James Stevens No.3' arrived at Grimsby on 23rd October 1898. She was moored in the

Grimsby Lifeboat "Manchester Unity"
1894 - 1904

Royal Dock Basin, and became an attraction for all to see. At the meeting of the local Lifeboat Committee held at Mr. Bannister's office on 26th October 1898, Captain Holmes extolled the virtues of the splendid new steam lifeboat, she had attained $8^1/_2$ knots on the voyage from Cowes, Isle of Wight, and she was fitted with a 'White' tubular boiler with compound steam mechanism, she consumed $2^1/_2$ cwts. of coal per hours. Captain Holmes thought that she would be an asset to Grimsby and the Fishing Industry would be reassured by the boat's presence.

Captain Holmes also informed the committee that written applications had been received for the position of Coxswain and after careful consideration it had been decided to appoint Mr. J. J. Platt for the job, and Mr. J. Ward as 2nd Coxswain. George Charlton was appointed Coxswain of the conventional boat.

It was decided to engage a nighwatchman to keep a vigilant eye on the lifeboat and lifeboat house, the Hon. Secretary to have full powers to order the lifeboat movements. As for advance warnings of the services of the lifeboat being required, 2 sound rockets to be fired for the 'Manchester Unity' and 4 sound rockets to be fired for the 'James Stevens No.3'.

The steam lifeboat was an attractive crowd puller, the local RNLI committee encouraged visitors to admire the impressive looking vessel from the jetty, no one was allowed aboard. As previously mentioned, she was moored in the Royal Dock Basin where she could be available in a very short time, her long low hull and twin funnels placed side by side belied her power, her raked mast and striking lines were a complete departure from the usual design of lifeboats.

The 'James Stevens No.3' was based at Grimsby for 5 years, being called out for service on 6 occasions but she was not called to save any lives.

In the small hours of January 7th 1900, reports came in that a large schooner had grounded near Spurn Point. The 'James Stevens' raised steam and at 3.40am proceeded to the scene. The schooner was identified as the 'Demarius' of Goole laden with a cargo of chalk and she had run aground off Spurn Point in heavy seas and gale force winds. When the Grimsby boat reached Spurn to assist the Spurn lifeboat (which was operated by the Hull Trinity House) the steam lifeboat stood by to give assistance if required. The 'Demarius' refloated at around 7am on the rising tide, some of the Grimsby lifeboat crew went aboard the schooner and managed to sail her into Grimsby Docks.

Captain Holmes had reported to the local committee of the RNLI a very serious matter concerning the behaviour of the crew of the 'Manchester Unity'. It appeared that in spite of adequate exercise with the lifeboat, the crew had no faith in the 2nd Coxswain. It was revealed that the lifeboat had run aground twice in 1899 and the crew blamed the 2nd Coxswain's incompetence for the incidents, the crew were adamant that they did not wish to sail with Mr. Grant and in view of this matter Mr. Grant was asked to resign and the Secretary was asked to recommend a suitable replacement for the position.

The local RNLI committee held their meeting at the Dock Offices on August 10th 1900, it was a very lively affair and was mainly about the antics of the Coxswain George Charlton and his drunken adventure with the 'Manchester Unity'. Apparently Charlton had been on a monumental drinking session, he had been drinking all day and had been thrown out of a pub at Lock Hill, he had staggered down to the Dock Basin. He cast a bleary eye round to see what his drunken state of mind could inspire, he enlisted the help of two men and they tried to launch the lifeboat. With an effort, the 'Manchester Unity' moved down the slip and hit the water with an almighty splash, nearly drowning Charlton, who was huddled up under the whaleback. He tried to steer her out of the basin, but only succeeded in going in circles as she had no way on her. She drifted aimlessly all over the Basin, luckily the crew of the 'James Stevens No.3' noticed the commotion and as they had some steam pressure they rescued the now sleepy Charlton from an unknown fate. As the steam lifeboat slipped her moorings to go to Charlton's aid, the 'Manchester Unity' collided with a shrimp boat and sank it. After some difficulty the crew of the steam lifeboat managed to go aboard the 'Manchester Unity' and haul the now unconscious Coxswain into the other boat and convey him ashore.

For these disgraceful events, George Charlton was dismissed from the RNLI who recorded their strongest feelings in the minutes. The Secretary was instructed to pay the owner of the shrimp boat, which was later raised, at the cost of £5.

Captain Jewitt had resigned owing to ill health, Lt. Jackson, who had performed valuable effort for the RNLI accepted Captain Jewitt's job as Secretary. Thanks and appreciation for Captain Jewitt's past work were recorded in the minutes.

In appalling gale force winds and mountainous seas the steam lifeboat on August 3rd 1900 left the Dock Basin to go to the assistance of Ketch 'Thomas and Mary' of Scarborough, but as the big steam boat tried to get out of the Dock Basin, she collided with the 5 ton fishing boat 'Elsie' of Grimsby. The 'Elsie' was so badly damaged that she was regarded as a total loss and full compensation was paid to the owner Mr. P. Anderson, in fact the lifeboat never left the Dock Basin that day owing to the incident. It is to be hoped that maybe the Spurn Point lifeboat assisted the Ketch on that occasion; the 'James Stevens' suffered superficial damage to ther bow and she returned to her moorings at about 2.15am.

At the local committee meeting of the RNLI held at Mr. Bannister's office on January 8th 1901, members were informed of the steam lifeboat's call out to the aid of a large four masted barque, later identified as the 'Lizbeth' of Hamburg which was in distress near the Haile Sand, the weather was appalling, a north westerly gale and frequent snow showers. The lifeboat steamed out to the vessel which had, apparently been under tow to Newcastle when the weather deteriorated and the crew had slipped the tow and dropped anchor, intending to ride out the storm. Unfortunately, the anchor dragged and the barque had drifted close to the treacherous Haile Sands. The tugs had left her at anchor thinking she would be safe until the following morning. The 'James Stevens' stood by for several hours until the weather moderated, eventually after assuring that the barque was in no danger, the vessel was reclaimed by the tugs and resumed her voyage.

The committee were informed of a letter from Commander St. Vincent Nepean of the London office, in which he advised that the high cost of operating the steam lifeboat would have to be lived with for the time being, and after discussion the committee agreed. Commander Nepean was concerned about the difficulties encountered by the lifeboat 'Manchester Unity' getting out of the Dock Basin in bad weather. Invariably a tug would be around to tow the boat out into the river but in high seas and storms this was not possible, thus reducing the availability of the service. In view of these circumstances his advice was to close the Grimsby Lifeboat Station and transfer the equipment to Spurn where a lifeboat had been in operation since 1810.

The problem of the continued differences of opinion between two members of the crew of the steam boat, (they were first and second Coxswains) and were Messrs. Schlanders and Melville. They just couldn't see eye to eye at all, a situation that affected the lifeboat's operation. It was resolved that Melville would be moved to another position in the local operation of the RNLI.

The 'Manchester Unity' was sent to Spurn Point in 1901, being loaned to the Hull Branch of Trinity House while a new lifeboat was being built for Spurn Point, their lifeboat having been withdrawn from service.

Again, at the local committee meeting of the RNLI held on 11th October 1902, tales were related of more discontent. The Coxswain and the Chief Engineer were always arguing and fighting, making the service nearly impotent. This state of affairs could not continue. The Coxswain was held to blame and so was dismissed, Mr. J. Hudson taking over as Coxswain.

On 14th January 1903, the local RNLI committee were told that the 'James Stevens No.3' had been sent to Gorleston for evaluation trials for 3 months. She was never to return.

The 'Manchester Unity' had returned from Spurn Point and was now water berthed in the Royal Dock, a new crew was to be formed to man her.

It was agreed that a sub-committee should be created to meet the RNLI Architect and the Engineer to give

Steam Lifeboat 'James Stevens 3' at Gorleston after leaving Grimsby c.1904.
Graham Farr Archives RNLI.

advice on a suitable site in the Royal Dock.

By now the committee were pressing for a new modern lifeboat as they regarded the 'Manchester Unity' as out of date and old fashioned. Some members of the committee had visited several Ports to look at other types of lifeboats that would be suitable for use at Grimsby. After consideration it was agreed to select the 'Liverpool' type of boat, this vessel would have both oars and a sail. She was of shallow draft and thus more effective in the Humber Estuary, she was fitted with water ballast tanks, which the Coxswain didn't think were necessary, but he agreed that on the whole, the 'Liverpool' type of lifeboat was the one for Grimsby.

It was reported to the Committee that the new slipway had been damaged by the Lowestoft Lugger 'Boy Victor' which had collided with the slip. A claim for insurance damage had been lodged with the relevant Company, it was agreed that a 'Dolphin' should be placed on the nearside of the ramp.

The 'Manchester Unity's' days at Grimsby were now numbered. In June 1904 she was replaced by a new 'Liverpool' type lifeboat, it should be noted that the 'Manchester Unity' had provided valuable service in the 11 years that she had been based at Grimsby and now she was to go, remembered by many as the lifeboat that performed good feats of rescue services for the benefit of local mariners.

The new boat was a non-self righting vessel built by the Thames Ironworks at a cost of £1,044. This lifeboat was provided out of a bequest of the late Charles T. M. Burton and she was so named 'Charles Burton' in his memory. To accommodate the new boat, which was 38ft long and 10ft 9 inches beam, a new boathouse and slipway were constructed near No.1 Fish Dock Lock Pit at a cost of £1,436.

The first call out to service for the 'Charles Burton' came on November 9th 1906. The barque 'Marie Becker' of Hamburg had run aground just near the Fish Docks at a time when the weather was fine and it was possible for small boats to go alongside and begin unloading her cargo. Everything was trouble free, the cargo was being moved without any difficulty. However, during the night the wind got up to gale force and the two men, who had remained on board the barque decided that they needed help. The vessel was stirring on the mud bank and several rivets started and she began taking water. The pumps could comfortably control the ingress of water but the two men were understandably anxious and signalled for help. The 'Charles Burton' was launched at 8.30am and took both men off. The 'Marie Becker' was refloated a few days later when necessary attention had been given to her leaky hull.

Meanwhile, Captain Boothby had been appointed Secretary of the local RNLI Branch Committee, Lt. Hall, the current Inspector of Lifeboats, announced that the Lifeboat Fund had ceased, but the Parent Committee (London) wanted to continue the annual collection. Lt. Hall suggested that the Saturday Lifeboat Committee should be allowed to elect 10 members to the local RNLI Group, he then pointed out that Rule No.1 of the RNLI stated that the local RNLI Committee should be elected annually.

The Grimsby lifeboat was launched to service at 10am on 5th February 1909, as a fishing smack was observed to be in difficulties and drifting out of control. The 'Charles Burton' found her near the Bull Light Vessel and identified her as the Grimsby vessel 'Providence'. It transpired that she had lost her sails in the full

Lifeboat-house built at Grimsby in 1903, used until 1927.

RNLI Grimsby Lifeboat 'Charles Burton' giving a demonstration in the Royal Dock Basin, Grimsby. c.1908

force of a north easterly gale, the weather was still very wintry and the lifeboat had had a stormy journey to assist the 'Providence'. However, the 'Charles Burton' managed to secure a line to the casualty and tow her back to port.

August 10th 1911 saw the Annual General Meeting of the local RNLI Lifeboat Committee, held in the Town Hall in Grimsby. This was a favourite social event and drew most of the Captains of Industry and their wives to join in the evening's events. All the Civic dignataries were there and when everyone had settled down, the local RNLI Inspector, Lt. Hall, addressed the meeting. He outlined the past years events and then came the election of the local committee.

The Countess of Yarborough was elected President of the Branch, the Chairman was Mr. E. Bannister, Vice Chairman Col. A. Bannister, and the rest of the commit-

tee was made up of upper class people plus the Vicar of Grimsby.

It was agreed to form a special committee and a suggestion made was for collecting boxes to be placed on ALL trawlers and fishing vessels, also a collecting box should be permanently positioned on the Pay Clerk's desk so that 'voluntary' payments could be made by crews signing off.

At the local committee meeting held on September 12th 1912 at Mr. Bannister's office, members were told that the Coxswain, Mr. J. Hudson, was retiring owing to his age (67). It was decided that he should receive a pension in recognition of his sterling service record. The Second Coxswain Bretton was appointed Coxswain, he had been a member of the crew for some time and had been popular with his mates and had shown himself to have the correct qualities of leadership necessary to justify his selection as Cox. Captain Baxter, the current RNLI Inspector, spoke of the interviews and assessment of candidates for the position of 2nd Coxswain and he recommended Mr. J. Smith. The committee agreed.

An Accountant, Mr. Curtis, agreed to audit the RNLI books for the agreed sum of 10/6 per annum. The Chairman then presented Mr. Hudson with a framed Certificate of Service, he also gave a glowing resume of Mr. Hudson's career in the RNLI service and finally told him that the RNLI Parent Committee had agreed to reward him with a pension of £7-5-0 per annum.

Mr. Hudson thanked the Chairman and Committee and offered his continued service to the RNLI.

The Secretary reported that the Royal Dock Basin had been dredged, Commander Rowley (of the London Committee visiting Grimsby) mentioned that the Management Committee were considering stationing a motor lifeboat at Spurn Point and they thought that such a craft would be much more efficient and manageable than the current sailing and rowing lifeboat used at Grimsby and Spurn Point. The Secretary was urged to proceed with the installation of a telephone at his house.

The first call out to service for the new Coxswain came on 31st October 1912. Several of the local fishing fleet had been caught up in a northerly gale that had sprung up. The seas had whipped up to turmoil and the 'Charles Burton' was called out about 12.20pm to stand by them as necessary. Luckily there were no untoward moments and the fishing smacks were able to cautiously make their way back to port under the watchful eye of the Grimsby lifeboat.

At a meeting of the local RNLI Branch Committee held at the secretary's office on June 5th 1914, it was reported that the secretary had had a telephone installed at his home. A letter of apology had been received from the Vicar of Grimsby, Canon A. A. Markham. Mr. Pearson, the assistant secretary, said that Cornflower Day had been a big success. Letters of condolence had been sent to Mesdames Sutcliffe and Davis in respect of the sad loss of their husbands. It was agreed to place the collecting boxes in the Dock Offices at Immingham and also in ships visiting the Port. Lt. Jackson (the Lifeboat Inspector) stated that under a RNLI regulation, a winchman had to be appointed to every lifeboat and it was suggested that Mr. Hudson, the retired Coxswain, should be appointed for the job at a reward of £1 per year. The secretary also mentioned that he was trying to get a telephone link established between Grimsby and Spurn Point. The Management Committee had agreed to a motor lifeboat being stationed at Spurn Point but the RNLI had advised that owing to a great demand it could be 2 years at least before such a craft would be available.

The use of a rocket alarm system being used to summon the lifeboat crew for call-out would be discontinued for the time being, the International situation being very worrying.

A meeting of the local RNLI Branch Committee held on July 23rd 1915 in the secretary's office was told that Lt. Jackson was now on Active Service. A temporary secretary, Capt. W. R. Brown was appointed. The special effects committee would still function and had raised a lot of money for the war effort. It was agreed that lifeboat practices should continue and perhaps such practices could coincide with a special efforts collection. Canon A. A. Markham, the Vicar of Grimsby, did not seem to attend many meetings, but he always sent his apologies by letter.

On February 23rd 1916 at 6am, the 'Charles Burton' was called out to assist HMS 'Violet' but when the lifeboat found the ship, no assistance was needed. The weather at this time was bitterly cold with a gale force wind and heavy seas running. This abortive call out did not help the crew's morale, a wasted journey requiring back breaking effort only to be waved away. Such was the lot of lifeboat crews on, fortunately, rare occasions. This time however, as a result of the adverse weather conditions, one of the crew was to lose his life. Henry Little caught a severe cold which brought on complications from which he died.

The Grimsby lifeboat was called out at 1.30am on March 16th 1916 to go to the assistance of 4 pile driving barges that were moored off the fish docks. The weather was appalling with mountainous seas, a gale force wind and heavy snow showers. The 'Charles Burton' stood by the barges until the weather improved and finally returned to her station some 15 hours later, another case of dedication to the job in hand.

During the Hostilities of 1914-1918, the RNLI lifeboat service carried on regardless of the increased danger from U-Boats, mines, and other difficulties that one would encounter in wartime conditions.

There would seem to be a lack of information regarding the 'Charles Burton's' duties during the Great War. Certainly the RNLI was as active throughout and it was well known that there were coastal defences near and at the Humber mouth and the Bull and Haile Forts during both World Wars. Apparently 5 crew members were called up on active service in 1916 and volunteers had to be found to make up the crew.

Also in 1916 the District Inspector reported that he had visited the Lifeboat Station and had gone out on practice in the lifeboat. He was impressed with the crew and the general efficiency and cleanliness of the station. Praise indeed, especially during wartime conditions. Collecting boxes had been allowed on Minesweepers and other HM Ships.

At the meeting of the local committee of the RNLI held in the secretary's office on February 5th 1918, a letter was read out from a Mr. Solomon who was the organising secretary of the local RNLI. He wanted MORE money!!! Mr. B. Fenner was appointed assistant secretary (poor chap, he had already carried out the secretary's duties unofficially for years, now it was official).

Early in December 1918, the 'Charles Burton' was called out to the assistance of the Grimsby fishing vessel 'Shamrock' which was in difficulties near the River mouth. The lifeboat sailed out to the scene of the trouble and found the 'Shamrock' minus her sail and drifting towards the shoals. The lifeboat managed to get a line aboard the 'Shamrock' and proceeded to tow her back to Grimsby without event. The owner of the vessel sent a letter of appreciation to the RNLI committee.

In the late afternoon of January 14th 1919, the 'Charles Burton' was launched to go to the assistance to a distress call from a vessel that appeared to be in trouble close to the infamous Middle Binks gravel banks near Spurn. The weather at the time was extremely bad, very rough seas, a S.S.E. gale and torrential rain reduced visibility considerably. The 'Charles Burton' left the Royal Dock Basin at about 4.30pm and proceeded to the ship in distress which turned out to be the ketch 'Semper Spera' of Rotterdam, bound from Boulogne to Hull. She was approximately in the middle of the shoals and it seemed a considerable time before Coxswain Bretton could manoeuvre alongside the ketch, but at last the lifeboat made it and took the exhausted crew of 4 off. Some of the crew of the 'Charles Burton' went aboard the ketch after a tug arrived and took the 'Semper Spera' in tow back to Grimsby.

On October 5th 1920, a meeting of the local branch committee decided to press the London Committee of Management to provide a motor lifeboat, as the present sailing boat, the 'Charles Burton', was very dependent on the wind and tide. In other words, out of date.

It was also proposed that the local Sea Scouts should be employed as signallers, thus helping the lifeboat crew, this proposition was carried out but the idea was abandoned later as the parents of the boys concerned had doubts about their safety at sea. Commander Carver was now Inspector of Lifeboats and had inspected the Lifeboat Station and had gone out with the crew on exercise and had expressed his satisfaction.

The difficulties of convincing people to serve on the local RNLI Committee was emphasised, during the early 1920's. Whether the local committee's image was one of social climbing and that precluded other more humble members of the public joining in it is hard to explain. However, a lot of people did a lot of essentially good work and credit should be given to everyone who took on the thankless jobs that were so necessary.

In November 1925 R. W. Long was appointed 1st Coxswain in place of R. B. Farrow who had retired, Captain W. Senior, who was the Port Master, had been appointed to the committee to begin an association with the RNLI that continued with his son Edward (who also became Port Master and also gave sterling service to the local and National RNLI). The Senior family served the

RNLI for over 60 years of continued involvement, a fine example of loyalty and dedication that not many families can beat.

Meanwhile the 'Charles Burton' had been launched at 8.35pm on January 21st 1924 to attend the steam crawler 'Loroone' of Grimsby that had run aground on the Binks. The lifeboat was towed out into the river by the tug 'Lynx'. The weather was pretty bad, a short choppy sea and a strong south easterly breeze which did not help. Apparently the 'Lynx' towed the lifeboat all the way out to the scene, what a bonus for the crew! They found the 'Loroone' aground as described, and stood by until the tide turned and luckily the trawler floated off undamaged and headed back to Grimsby. Then the lifeboat was towed back to her station by the 'Lynx' arriving about 5am.

To bring the Cleethorpes and Grimsby part of the 'Lifeboats of the Humber' to a close, we have seen the beginnings of the lifeboat service bring reassurance and help to the fishing fleet. We have seen the lifeboat's presence accepted and welcomed, both at Cleethorpes and Grimsby. Many lives were saved, many rescues attempted, some successful, some not.

In the 45 years during the stationing of lifeboat facilities in Grimsby, the lifeboats were launched 40 times on service and 19 lives were saved.

The end of an era seemed to be fading when the Lifeboat Station closed but was it?

Extract from the Grimsby News of May 6th 1927:-

Regarding the discontinuance of the Lifeboat Station, we have been handed by Captain Boothby a letter which he has received from the Secretary of the Royal National Lifeboat Institution. This letter which we give below

RNLI Grimsby Lifeboat 'Charles Burton' 1904 - 1927 on exercise in the Royal Dock Basin, Grimsby. c.1920

speaks for itself. "Sir - The Committee of Management have now decided, with the full concurrence of the Grimsby Trawler Owners and other interested in shipping, that the lifeboat which was stationed at the Port in 1868, is no longer needed under present conditions, and that the Station should, therefore, be closed.

As you know, the Institution has not acted precipitately in this matter, which has indeed, been under consideration for over two years. But the establishment of one of our most powerful motor lifeboats at Spurn Point on the Humber and the other arrangements made on the coast, are regarded as fully meeting the requirements of the case as regards shipping entering and leaving the Humber and the Institution, which provides the lifeboats service around the whole of the Coasts of the United Kingdom is, as you know, gradually, but steadily reducing the number of its pulling and sailing boats in proportion as it develops its scheme of guarding the strategic points with powerful motor boats.

The step now taken will, therefore, undoubtedly meet with the full approval of all those interested in the lifeboat service as a great national undertaking, and the Committee of Management feel sure that they may look with confidence to the inhabitants of Grimsby, and especially to those engaged in, and connected with shipping (and more particularly with the Trawling Industry), to support this great national service as generously as possible. For, in doing so, they will be assisting to maintain a service which, for over a hundred years, has, in peace and war alike, come to the rescue of mariners of all nations, but, as might be expected, especially to the rescue of British seafarers. In that period over 60,800 lives have been rescued.

The Port of Grimsby will do honour to itself and to a great national and heroic cause by placing the Town in its legitimate position in the list of Cities and Towns throughout the United Kingdom which accord generous support to the Red Cross of the Sea, and we are confident that both the Institution and the Town of Grimsby will have the advantage of your support and personal sympathy in achieving a high place on that list. Yours faithfully. (Signed) George F. Shee, Secretary. Commander H. B. Boothby DSO RNR, Grimsby Branch.

CHAPTER TWO

LIFEBOATS AT SPURN POINT 1810-1908

In 1789, an entrepreneurial boat builder called Henry Greathead residing in South Shields decided to build a 'Lifeboat' which he was certain would aid and assist 'mariners' in distress. His design was for a boat of perhaps 30ft by 9ft beam with a whaleback at either end thus enabling it to be rowed in each direction, having in effect a bow at each end. This design turned out to be potentially viable and Mr. Greathead realised that he could have a winner in his hands.

To promote his design and to enhance his business, he prepared a brochure which he sent to a selection of coastal towns to 'test the waters'. It would appear that Mr.

Greathead's idea and design attracted a fair amount of interest, as the Towns of Ayr and Aberdeen ordered lifeboats from him.

A newspaper in Hull heard of Mr. Greathead's idea and published an article on the subject with a suggestion that such a boat stationed at the Humber mouth would serve a much needed purpose. Mr. Greathead must have had a very efficient news gathering service because he soon heard of the newspaper's suggestions. He quickly wrote to the Elder Brethren of the Hull Trinity House on October 22nd 1802 explaining his design and enclosing his brochure and prices. Keen to obtain business, he

The "Original" lifeboat built by Greathead, launched at South Shields in 1789. From engraving by Finden.

offered to supply a boat for the same price that he had quoted Ayr and Aberdeen. He explained that his boat could be rowed either way without the boat having to be turned around and that this design was a breakaway from the traditional transom stern rowing boat.

Shortly after Mr. Greathead's design hit the headlines, Lloyds of London, having studied the idea, decided to back it and published a report stating that the potential of this type of craft was so exciting that they had set aside £2,000 to encourage the establishing of lifeboats around the coast of Great Britain. They furthermore gave the entrepreneurial Mr. Greathead 100gns as a tribute to his foresight, skill and ability. Mr. Greathead's brochure, which he sent to the Brethren at Hull Trinity House, stated that for £130 one could buy an 8 oared lifeboat of his design and a 10 oared boat would cost £150.

Trinity House records reveal that the Brethren had had exhaustive trials carried out on boats of Mr. Greathead's design and they certainly performed well.

On March 7th 1803, Mr. Iveson, who, was the steward to Mr. Francis Constable of Burton Constable near Hull, and who was Lord of the Manor of the Spurn area, wrote to Hull Trinity House agreeing to the establishment of a lifeboat at Spurn Point. Mr. Iveson stated that if this could be done he thought the indicated difficulty of obtaining sufficient men to man the boat could be overcome by persuading such men to come in from Kilnsea. Mr. Constable would be pleased to help in any way.

It would appear that the Brethren of Hull Trinity House deliberated on this matter for a long time. Records tell us that on April 7th 1810 Mr. Iveson wrote again to the Brethren on Mr. Constable's behalf to emphasise his enthusiasm and desire to see a lifeboat at Spurn Point, and that he had the shell of a building which had previously been used as an Army barracks but could be converted for use of the Master and crew of the proposed lifeboat, also some accommodation could be made for the use of rescued people.

Mr. Iveson also said that Mr. Constable was willing to erect a boathouse if Trinity House would supply the measurements of the lifeboat when it was obtained plus, of course, the essential carriage which would carry the boat to the water.

Mr. Constable would provide 12 able bodied men to be available as the crew of the lifeboat. He would offer a means of livelihood for the Master of the boat and for the mate if this was considered necessary. Mr. Constable was willing to do all this at his own expense such was his desire and enthusiasm. However, he thought that the commercial and shipping interests at Hull should pay for the boat and that the Brethren of Hull Trinity House should be the appropriate body to handle the project, select the Master, oversee the establishment and settle salvage claims.

The means of livelihood for the Master was to be the managing of the Tavern which was to be a part of the facilities at Spurn Point. He would sell poultry, vegetables, and provisions to vessels (numbering approx. 500 a year) that came to Spurn to ballast with cobbles and gravel. The Master would also cater for the labourers and any visitors who came from time to time. Mr. Iveson said that the 12 able bodied men who were to man the lifeboat would come from Kilnsea.

The Brethren of Hull Trinity House decided to start a subscription right away to defray the cost of the boat and the maintenance of the establishment at Spurn.

They wrote again to Mr. Greathead asking for his brochure, prices and details of delivery etc., he replied almost immediately, suggesting a strong 10 oared boat which would cost £200 although he could supply an 8 oared boat which would be lighter for £165. The Brethren by this time knew what they wanted and they ordered the 10 oared boat and asked for measurements and those of the carriage so they could pass them on to Mr. Constable to help him with the construction of the boathouse.

The response to the subscription was swift and very agreeable. By June 20th about £300 had been raised, of which the Brethren gave £50, Lloyds of London gave the same and the Corporation of the City of Hull also chipped in with £50.

Meanwhile, the Brethren interviewed the applicants for the position of Master. Mr. Iveson informed them that the conversion of the building at Spurn were continuing apace.

The Tavern would be supplied with coal, candles, and a spy glass, a flag pole and flag, and 6 casks for the storage of water. The Master's earnings should total at least £100 from which concessions totalling £47-10-0 would be deducted. If for some reason the Master failed to earn £100 per year, any shortfall would be made up to that figure by Mr. Constable.

The use of the flag would be to assemble the people in the neighbourhood so that help could be administered to the rescued whom it was reasoned would need immediate attention.

Mr. Greathead informed Trinity House on August 15th 1810 that the lifeboat was almost complete. The Brethren had, after due consideration of all the other applicants, decided to appoint Robert Richardson Master of the Lifeboat and Master of the Tavern.

About the middle of September, the Brethren arranged with Messrs. Hewson to use their Brig 'Thomas' to tow the lifeboat from South Shields to Hull for the sum of £10, the contractors to pay £200 if the lifeboat was lost en route.

Subscriptions by now had reached nearly 430 gns, which was very satisfactory. The Brig 'Thomas' left South Shields with the lifeboat in tow on October 2nd and arrived without incident in Hull a few days later. The Brethren at once gave the order for the carriage to be constructed for the estimated sum of £50 but as numerous alterations and changes in the design were deemed necessary, the final amount to pay was £84-2. The carriage was an impressive sight, the lifeboat was to be carried between two 16ft wheels.

It was delivered at Spurn on October 29th 1810, but the boathouse was not ready, in fact the carriage house had not been completed. The lifeboat, however, soon found employment when she was called out for the first time to go to the assistance of the 'John and Charlotte' of Newcastle when she ran aground on the Trinity sand in a gale.

The word 'assistance' is often used to describe the lifeboat's duties, but if one looks behind the word and try to realise the battles with the wind and waves that confront every lifeboat, one is aware of the howling gale, the mountainous seas, the strength needed to pull on the oars, the frustration even when the lifeboat is literally picked up and flung back from the stricken ship. The soaked, sweating crew in their oilskins and sou'westers, the sheer exhaustion that sets in, but also the sense of achievement that comes through when the crew of a stranded vessel are safely landed, then some brief relaxation for the lifeboat men could be enjoyed.

Sometimes a rescue could be straightforward, and a grounded ship could be refloated without damage or difficulty, sometimes some of the cargo had to be jettisoned to lighten the ship, conversely, on occasions sand has to be dug away from the grounded ship to allow a channel to enable her to float free. This could be back breaking work but often necessary.

When at last the carriage arrived at Spurn it was found to be too big for the boathouse, or the boathouse was too small for the carriage so the structure was altered accordingly.

The Brethren were administering the lifeboat station very well. They looked after the interests of the Master and his crew and they dealt with salvage claims demanded from the owners of craft that had been given assistance by the lifeboat. The Brethren then shared out the salvage money among the Master and crew. In March 1813, the rewards for two incidents of rescue were £7 and £9. In December of the same year the Brethren instructed Mr. Ringrose, who owned the 'Sir Peter', to pay 100gns for help given when the vessel ran aground on the Stony Binks at the mouth of the Humber. The lifeboatmen got £10, the crew of two other ships who also helped got £90 and the Brethren of Hull Trinity house paid £5 into the poor box at Trinity House.

On occasions, an award of £20 was divided into shares of 25 shillings for each of the crew. The Master received £2-10-0, the same amount went into the fund for maintaining the boat and Brethren also put a small amount into their poor box but in some cases after amounts had been received from salvage monies, the Brethren would cover their maintenance costs only.

Records of the Brethren of Hull Trinity House reveal

accounts of bravery and courage shown by the lifeboat crew and they are praised accordingly.

The Brethren wrote to Mr. Constable in April 1816 to suggest that cottages should be built at Spurn for the crew, as they had to travel from their homes in neighbouring villages maybe 3 or 4 miles distant and this was causing delays in getting the lifeboat away to a rescue. The Brethren thought that if the crew were resident at Spurn the smooth running attributes of the lifeboat operation would be greatly enhanced and the money that the crew earned from ballasting ships would enable them to pay rent for the cottages.

Mr. Iveson, who answered the letter, replied that Mr. Constable, who was now 63 years old, did not want to be involved in any further business arrangements but he would be willing to lease as much land as required for the construction of the cottages at a 'Peppercorn' rent, if the Brethren would build them.

On November 25th 1818, the Brethren started the subscription list to raise money for the construction of the cottages. They, themselves, started the ball rolling with £50 and the shipping interests in Hull gave the same amount, the public contributed generously as they obviously realised what a good job the lifeboat crew were doing.

The result of the fund raising for the building of the cottages at Spurn was a good one, over £800 having been subscribed, a lot of money in those days!!!

On January 2nd 1819, Mr. Constable granted a 21 year lease on the land at Spurn for the building of 12 cottages at a nominal rent of 5 shillings per year. The building of the cottages began immediately and they were soon fit for habitation, the crew were housed where their work was and were readily available for lifeboat duties. On April 27th 1821, the Master of the Lifeboat reported to the Trinity House Brethren that his crew had been beaten up by ruffians, who stole the cobbles and stones for themselves and were supplying other vessels with ballast. This was a serious matter and the Brethren received a report from Mr. Iveson on behalf of Mr. Constable reassuring the Master and crew that they had the exclusive rights to dig the cobbles and stones for ballasting vessels.

On June 8th 1821, the Troopship 'Thomas' was driven onto the Stony Binks, the Lifeboat Master's report of the accident was as follows:-

"On Friday morning 8th, inst. about half past one o'clock am, the wind being east north east strong breeze, I saw a vessel on the Binks but saw no signal of distress. I immediately mustered the crew of the lifeboat, launched her and went to the vessel. She proved to be the 'Thomas' of London, a Transport No.40, bound of Hull with twenty six troops and an Officer (Major Tovey) on board, the Master of the ship asked me if I would take an anchor out. I told him I could make no bargains of that nature, the preservation of their lives was my object as the ship was in a very dangerous situation and could not possible get off. I then offered to take all the people into the lifeboat and carry them to shore and said if I afterwards found carrying an anchor out would be of any service I would endeavour to do it.

I then took the troops with Major Tovey into the lifeboat by means of a sling from the main yard. The agent, Lt. Pritchard, said the troops might go but he felt himself bound to stay by the ship with the crew, as the Pilot had told them there was no danger.

I then, it being about 4 o'clock, put the troops and Major Tovey on board the 'BEE' Revenue Cutter which was cruising near by and remained with the boat at the edge of the breakers.

The crew of the ship were at this time pumping very hard at both pumps and continued pumping until 11 o'clock when the ship filled with water. The crew then hoisted a signal of distress at the peak end and took to the main and mizzen riggings and as soon as I observed the signal, I immediately tried to get to the ship and with great difficulty got to the larboard bow and hailed them to let go the stopper and shank painter and let go the anchor lest it should stove the lifeboat. I then let go the lifeboat's anchor, the sea being very heavy. All the ship's boats had been previously washed away but we succeeded getting the whole of the crew, 26 in number, with two women and a child much exhausted into the lifeboat about 12 o'clock.

The wreck of the Thomas. The lifeboat is depicted along with the BEE Revenue Cutter (right). Pilot boat No.6, the Duke of Wellington, appears far left with No.5, Rover, on the right and No.4, Fox, in the distance.
Hull City Museums and Art Galleries.

The Captain of the ship, Lieutenant Pritchard, and the Carpenter, with the two women were much bruised and hurt. I am sorry to say one woman was unfortunately drowned and that Lieutenant Pritchard nearly lost his life endeavouring to save her. There were six or seven of the crew overboard at the same time but all were saved. When I got a little way from the ship, a man was perceived in the mizzen rigging. I immediately put the crew on board the Pilot boat No.6 and returned to the ship and succeeded in bringing the man off whom I put on board the 'BEE' Revenue Cutter.

During the time I was employed in taking out the crew from the ship, the sea was breaking over her tops and I expected every moment her masts coming over her sides, which had they come, the lifeboat and crew together with the ship's crew must have perished and no boat could then approach the ship. I then returned on shore myself and

crew much exhausted having been in the boat nearly 11 hours the wind still E.N.E.

I am likewise sorry to say the lifeboat was much injured and stove."

R. Richardson.

We do hereby certify that the above statement or report of Robert Richardson the Master of the Lifeboat is in every particular correct and true.

Dated the 20th day of June, 1821.
S. P. Pritchard.
Lieut. and Agent afloat"

George Tovey.
Major 29th Command.

The Admiralty clearly appreciated the lifeboat's efforts concerning the rescue of the Troopship 'Thomas', for they granted the Master of the lifeboat 10gns and the crew were given 2gns each for their part in the rescue.

However, the crew's other activities took a knock when Mr. Iveson, on behalf of Mr. Constable, wrote to the Brethren saying "That in consequence of the reduction in the price of freights, labour and other conditions, it is necessary to reduce the wages for the loading of vessels with cobbles and gravel at Spurn. The wages have been 4/6 per man per tide, it is necessary to reduce them to 3/6 but I have doubts whether that price can be supported".

They were hard times indeed, and there was no recourse to the union in those days. Men were blatantly used and cast adrift at a whim, the very fact that they risked their lives to save others with the lifeboats was, in financial terms, inconsequential.

During 1821, 6 vessels were assisted when they ran aground near Spurn. During 1822, bad feeling between the Master and the lifeboat crew was very evident, 8 of the crew complained to the Brethren about Mr. Richardson's conduct in demanding his share of monies when he was not working with the men loading cobbles and gravel. When the men received their money by using the small boat they felt they were under obligation to spend their hard earned cash in his Public House, there being no alternative, and more serious, when any of the crew was taken ill, they were not given a share of the money earned.

The Brethren held a full investigation of the situation, which resulted in 6 of the crew being sacked and Richardson being warned as to his future conduct.

Dismissal must have been a grievous blow to a crew man, not only was he losing his jobs, his cottage went too and he and his family were literally out on the 'street', rough justice in those days.

In 1822, 6 vessels were given assistance by the lifeboat and her gallant crew. The Brethren were ready with their demands for salvage money due from assistance in time and need, the salvage money was shared out among the Master and crew, also the Trinity House Lifeboat Fund and the Brethren's poor box.

December 1823 was unique, if only for the fact that the lifeboat, which was moored instead of being in the Lifeboat House, broke loose from its moorings and was so badly thrown about in the violent gale that was raging at the time, that it overturned and sank, so severe was the damage that she was declared a complete wreck and was completely unserviceable.

The Brethren rose to the occasion and started a subscription for a new lifeboat. As an incentive to contribute, a long record of the lifeboat's services was placed near the subscription list, 34 vessels had been given help and assistance, 20 lives had been saved. The Brethren started things off with £100, the Mayor and Aldermen of Hull gave £50 on condition that, in future, the lifeboat would be under control of the Superintendent of a committee to consist of an equal number of members from the Corporation of the Mayor and Burgesses, The Trinity House and the Shipowners Society. They also stipulated that the boat would only be used for saving lives of people in ships wrecked or in difficulties, but NOT for preserving cargoes and could NOT assist in refloating vessels aground as had happened in the past.

A lot of stipulation for £50!!! and the Brethren threw the cumbersome conditions out, pointing out that they had successfully operated the lifeboat establishment for some 14 years.

Meanwhile, tenders were invited from boat builders from Scarborough, Whitby, Hull, Sunderland, and South Shields for the construction of a new lifeboat.

Ironically, the remains of the old lifeboat were sold to Thomas Mason, who as a boat builder of some repute in Hull, was to be awarded the tender for the new Spurn Lifeboat. The old boat was later converted into a shrimp boat for use in the river.

The new lifeboat cost approximately £190 and it was delivered to Spurn Point in the Summer of 1824, the measurements were 30ft long by 10ft beam and a draught of 3ft 7inches. Records mention that a vessel was assisted when aground near Spurn on October 10th but further information was not available.

The lifeboat continued the good work of aiding ships

in distress, mainly due to running aground. The crew were otherwise engaged in digging out cobbles and gravel for either making roads or ballasting vessels that put into Spurn for that purpose. The ballast business seemed to be quite profitable in 1821 and 1822, for the crew made £80 each in 1821, £60 each in 1822, and 1823, £39 each.

It would seem that from time to time quarrels broke out among the crew and men from neighbouring villages who had been recruited by Mr. Constable's agent when the ballast trade became too busy for the crew to handle. It was evident that the Spurn crew resented the other men being brought in to ease the work load and tempers got very frayed.

Records reveal accounts for November 1841 showing that A. G. Carte supplied 12 life preservers for use of the Spurn Lifeboat crew, at a cost of £7-4-0d. This would appear to be the first time that such safety equipment had been supplied to the crew.

It is also interesting to note that the leaflet sent to the Brethren advertising the life preservers describe Mr. Carte as 'Ordinance store keeper of the Citadel, Hull.'

It was about this time that the Brethren decided to retire Robert Richardson, the Master of the Lifeboat and of the Tavern, a controversial character but a good leader. He had reached retirement age and it was felt that a younger man was now necessary to carry out the duties. Robert Richardson had given 31 years outstanding service in a hard and arduous job. Under his leadership, 304 lives had been saved from wrecked vessels and his proud record shows that not one of the lifeboat crew had been lost during his time as Master.

Joseph Davey, aged 28, was appointed Master of the Lifeboat on the same terms as Mr. Richardson on December 4th 1841 and took up his residence at Spurn Point.

Records for 1842 show many repairs being carried out at the crew's cottages, and on November 23rd the Brethren increased the rent. The Master had to pay £2 per annum and the crew had to pay 12 shillings per year each. Unrest among the crew reared its ugly head soon after, men being absent from duty and some of the crew leaving unexpectedly and without giving forewarning or notice. These places having to be filled hurriedly and not always successfully.

On February 19th, the schooner 'Elizabeth' of Hartlepool, ran aground on the Stony Binks. After firing distress rockets without any response from the lifeboat, the crew then tried burning barrels of tar on the decks, again without any sign of the Spurn Lifeboat. Luckily, the 'Elizabeth' managed to refloat herself without any damage or loss of life and she proceeded on her voyage to Hull.

It was fortunate that the above mentioned vessel was able to refloat herself without any help. What happened to the lifeboat service will never be known, but had an enquiry been held, very serious repercussions would have echoed throughout the establishment at Spurn and the Hull Trinity House Brethren. However, the Brethren were, quite rightly, very concerned and drastic action was called for and taken.

Joseph Davey was removed as Master of the Lifeboat and dismissed, and Robert Brown, a master mariner, was appointed in his place.

The Spurn Lifeboat assisted several ships in difficulties and distress during 1843, but the earning capacity of the crew on the ballast workings decreased drastically as the supply of cobbles and gravel started to run out in the established areas around Spurn Point. Much of this commodity had been taken away to be used for making roads. The average earnings of the crew in the last half of the year was only 13/7 per week, the Master asked the Brethren to give some relief as by the following February 1844 their earnings had fallen to 9/8 a week and the Brethren agreed to give each man 4/- per week and each child 1/-.

On March 11th 1844, the crew of the lifeboat had two vessels aground at the same time in a dreadful gale. With difficulty the Master and crew took the people off both ships without loss of life.

The early tides of February 1845 were of abnormal height and they flooded the cottages causing great filth, misery and depression. To quote a report, "The water filled the house half way up the ovens, wet the beds, washed our fresh water away, the casks floating away, it broke the fencing, and washed away our coals and left the cottages in a very wretched condition.

"We expected every wave to burst the doors for it came with such fury that we had no time to secure anything, having to attend the crews of stranded vessels to get to shore with their boats, our wives and infants having to be upstairs without fires on account of the chimneys smoking and when they came down the floors were inches thick with mud that the water had brought in and left".

The Brethren were sympathetic and allowed each man £1 to help make good his loss. For quite a long time after this repair work was put in hand to restore the cottages to their former condition.

The expense of these repairs to the cottages and the maintenance of the boat and help given to the crew in times of calamity caused the Brethren to set up a committee to decide whether the lifeboat establishment was still necessary. Eventually the committee came back with their findings and said that they considered the lifeboat infinitely essential and necessary and since its inception in 1810 the Brethren of Hull Trinity House had given £780-19-7d to the upkeep. Up to 1838, 304 people having been saved from stricken ships, the last occasion resulted in 9 people having been saved from the wreck 'Fame', also since 1838, 21 vessels had been given assistance when becoming stranded.

After due consideration, the Brethren decided to adopt the report, but the earnings of the crew continued to dwindle as very little gravel was available and many vessels had to go away empty.

The Brethren continued to help financially with the crews earnings and their families. On September 6th 1848 Robert Brown, the Master of the Lifeboat and Tenant of the Tavern, applied for the renewal of his licence to sell liquor. The Chief Magistrate, the Rev. Christopher Sykes, told him that his licence was only to sell liquor on the Tavern premises and not on the beach or outside the property. If he was to disregard these regulations he would be prosecuted. Two weeks later Robert Brown informed the Brethren that he was being prevented from selling liquor to the ships when they called at Spurn for ballast. Mr. Brown felt that the present situation was impossible, and he couldn't make any sort of a living under the current circumstances so he intended to resign from his position of Master of the Lifeboat and Tenant of the Tavern on November 1st.

The Brethren appointed Michael Stanley Welburn as Master of the Lifeboat and tenant of the Tavern in Mr. Brown's place on November 1st 1848. The long suffering crew continued to man the lifeboat and they had occasion to approach the Brethren again for financial relief on account of their pitiful earnings. These cries from the heart came so often that the Brethren created a weekly payment system. In 1849 the Brethren set up a committee to obtain estimates for the possible renewing of the cottages which were showing signs of wear and tear. It was felt that some of the cottages were, perhaps, beyond economical repair. The financial obligation of maintaining the lifeboat establishment at Spurn was getting out of hand and the Brethren were concerned about the on going expenses which didn't seem to be getting less.

However, the Lifeboat Station was essential and on October 27th 1849, an order was made enabling the Brethren to provide a large amount of chalk to be used for the protection of the cottages and to do as much repair in other places at Spurn.

1850 brought an order from the Admiralty to prevent any further removal of gravel and shingle at Spurn-owing to the injurious effect to the estuary of the Humber. The digging of ballast and shingle was counter productive to the protection of the coastline at Spurn and the lighthouse against the erosion of the sea, but after second thoughts however, the Admiralty agreed to the crew working the gravel and shingle on the southern part of Spurn. A very sad day in the annals of the Spurn lifeboat service occurred on October 24th 1850 when the Brig 'Cumberland' of Newcastle had been driven ashore near Kilnsea in a violent storm and was breaking up in the mountainous seas. The lifeboat went to the assistance of the wreck and fired a rocket line to try to take the small lifeboat tender over to pick up the 'Cumberland's' crew, eventu-

An early Spurn lifeboatman complete with
cork lifebelt and jacket. c.1850
Town Docks Museum, Hull.

ally a line was got aboard the wreck and later 5 of the crew were taken off.

The next attempt to rescue the remaining men from the stricken vessel was not successful and a tragedy happened when one of the lifeboat crew, John Welburn, was drowned. Fortunately, a fishing smack was on hand and gave assistance thus enabling the remaining 9 men on the wreck to be taken ashore. A public subscription was set up to raise money for Mrs. Welburn and totalled £41.

December 1850 brought the news that the Brethren had decided to stop paying weekly amounts to the crew, who then wrote back to say as their earnings from salvage and loading ballast averaging 18/- per week were not sufficient to enable them to keep their families they would have to resign their positions and look elsewhere for employment. This statement of fact gave the Brethren much concern and a lot of thought was devoted to finding a solution to this serious problem. Eventually the Brethren resumed paying the relief money to the crew, this was 3/6 to single men and 5/- to married couples and 1/- to each child. Letters were sent to Shipping companies and other business houses asking for financial assistance to maintain the lifeboat establishment. In those letters, mention was made of the proud record of the lifeboat at Spurn, pointing out that since the lifeboat was stationed at Spurn in 1810, 729 lives had been saved.

A violent storm on March 5th and 6th 1851 with very high tides breached the peninsula in several places and undermined the low lighthouse, flooded several cottages and damaged the lifeboat which was moored instead of being in the lifeboat house.

All cobbles and gravel working was suspended and the crews now had no means of income at all. Desperation set in and some men packed up and left to go elsewhere for employment. The Brethren tried to help with small amounts of money and the crew were able to earn some money when they were able to unload stones from lighters brought in to mend the large gaps on the Peninsula at Spurn Point.

Things did however, seem brighter in June 1851 when the Admiralty gave permission for the crew to work cobbles and gravel from the southern most tip of Spurn but the gravel was very thin and hard to dig out.

Records reveal that much of the cobbles and stones were taken to Hull for the construction of roads and concrete.

On August 7th 1852, the Brethren decided to obtain a new lifeboat as the old one was showing ominous signs of wear. She had had a hard life and it was felt that a new one would be beneficial to the smooth operation of the lifeboat service. After studying tenders and estimates of various types of lifeboats, a contract was awarded to Messrs. Hallett of Hull for the sum of £112-18-6d.

Mr. M. Welburn, the Master of the Lifeboat, died in April 1853, and the Brethren expressed their profound regret. They decided to appoint John Calvert in his place as Master. He had served for 12 years as the mate on the Trinity House yacht and he was thought to be eminently suitable for the responsible position as Master of the Lifeboat and Licencee of the Lifeboat Inn, as it came to be named.

It became very apparent in 1853 that the condition of some of the cottages were deteriorating badly, not only were they some 30 years old but they had been flooded several times, which didn't do them any good at all. After thorough inspection, the Brethren ordered the three on the low ground to be demolished and 3 new ones to be built at the other end of the row.

It must be a tribute to the Masters and crews of the Spurn Point lifeboats that throughout the difficult years of near poverty for the crew when their income dried up owing to the ballast trade, they were always ready to man the lifeboat and go to the aid of some unfortunate crew of a grounded ship. Credit should also be given to the Brethren of Hull Trinity House who stood by the lifeboat establishment at Spurn Point when times were not so rosy and gave financial help to keep the wolf from the door of those brave, gallant men who manned the lifeboat.

Disaster at sea never finds an unacceptable level, just when things seem quiet, no one runs aground, every ship sails by. The emergence of steam propulsion, with its better control of movement and quicker response to the helm, meant the gradual end to the graceful lines of the sailing ship. Not so many steam ships grounded at Spurn, but the sailing ships still found the shallow shoals of the Binks and the sand banks existing in the Humber estuary. However, whoever had the misfortune to run aground at Spurn Point, always found the lifeboat would do their utmost to extend every effort to rescue the crew.

John Calvert was not destined to be Master of the Lifeboat for very long, for in December 1853, after only 9 months of service, he resigned his appointment and George Grant, who had been a fisherman all his working life in the Humber, took over.

The condition of the boathouse at Spurn was now giving cause for alarm, it had been battered by the waves and gales for 30 years and was literally falling apart. The Brethren had a good look at it and decided to build another one and after tenders had been invited and examined, one was found acceptable and was given to John Hamble on October 23rd 1854.

The Admiralty decided again to prohibit the digging or excavation of gravel and shingle from the coast and rivers of the United Kingdom.

The Brethren approached the Admiralty on behalf of the crew to try to get some concession but the Lords of the Admiralty were adamant. This again resulted in the loss of good men from the crew as they simply couldn't survive financially so they attempted to find work elsewhere and by September 1855 there were only 5 men left on the station.

Some months later the Admiralty relented somewhat and agreed to the crew working gravel and shingle on the Stony Binks!!!!

The Brethren, to their credit, were always looking for ways and means to give the lifeboat crews profitable employment. They thought they might have hit on a good idea, this was the possible setting up of fishing station at Spurn to provide the important extra income for the men. The Brethren were excited about the new possibility and placed an advert for men to show their interests in the scheme.

The Advert was as follows:-

WANTED

5 Fishermen, to supply the present vacancies in the crew of The Lifeboat Station at Spurn Point.

Each man will be allowed after the rate of £10 per annum and to have the occupation of the cottages at Spurn at a rent of 1/- per month, and also to share in the earnings of a fishing smack and boats which are used in collecting buoyage, in fishing at the entrance of the Humber and in rendering salvage to ships in distress.

The Master of the Lifeboat, George Grant, was lent £300 at 5% interest on the security of his fishing smack 'Phoebe' to buy or obtain the necessary equipment required for fishing. The new members of the crew were soon involved and once again the lifeboat station was found to be working together again.

But in November 19th 1855, a disaster overtook the lifeboat operation at Spurn. The lifeboat had gone to the aid of the schooner 'Zabina' which had run aground on the Binks. The weather was appalling, a violent storm raging and when attempting to take the crew of the 'Zabina' off into the lifeboat, she overturned and 2 members of the crew were drowned. They were Henry Holmes and John Combes. A subscription was opened to benefit the widows. Mrs. Holmes received £3-2-6! Records reveal that Henry Holmes had diced with death only a fortnight before when he was TWICE washed out of the lifeboat when she was assisting the Barque 'Sovereign' which was aground on the Binks. What significance is the saying 'Wooden Ships and Iron Men'? The Admiralty acknowledged Henry Holmes's bravery and gave his grieving widow £10, gratitude indeed!

Apparently when the lifeboat capsized, the Master and crew were rescued by the fishing Cobble 'York' of Filey.

Unfortunately, the fishing station project was not a success in spite of the efforts and determination of the crew. Men were coming and going and the replacements were not as always reliable as the long serving members of the crew. On May 6th 1856, some nine months after the start of the scheme, the number of men available to man the lifeboat was 8.

To correct this serious inbalance, the Brethren advertised for men for the lifeboat operation. They also resolved to pay the crew a monthly wage of £2-5-0 each and to divide the earnings of the lifeboat into 110 shares, 10 being for the upkeep of the lifeboat, 16 shares for the Master, 12 to the Mate, and the 8 men of the crew 9 shares each. In effect, this scheme does not seem to have received the enthusiasm that was expected. George Grant, the Master of the Lifeboat, left his position in the August and the Brethren after due consideration, appointed Richard Parrott as Master of the Lifeboat at a wage of £6 per month. William Long was the mate and he earned £4 per month and each crew man was now receiving £2-15-0 a month, the share scheme was to remain unaltered.

Meanwhile, the heavy seas and gales still wreaked their vengeance on the living accommodation at Spurn. In fact the damage was so bad that part of the Master's house and part of the Public House collapsed. The Brethren had to act quickly and their decision was to build new accommodation to the south west of the cottages and east of the lighthouse.

Approaches were made to Sir Clifford Constable for a lease on the site. Sir Clifford was sympathetic and agreed to the request. In February 1857, the Brethren had put out tenders for the construction of the cottages and eventually accepted the price from Messrs. Ellis and Johnson to erect the cottages for £1,300.

In August 1857, William Willis was appointed Master of the Lifeboat succeeding Richard Parrott. The crew moved into the new cottages early in 1858 and the Brethren breathed a sigh of relief, at last the crew would be housed in new, modern cottages, surely they could expect troublefree housing for many years!!! With the crew on regular monthly wages and reasonably content, the station seemed stable and content, in fact more settled than ever before.

Rescues continued and the lifeboat had to go to the aid of 4 Brigs that ran onto the Binks during a northerly gale and heavy seas on Guy Fawkes night 1858. Three of the vessels were refloated on the next tide but the remaining Brig was wrecked and broke up. However, the crews were saved and brought ashore. 1858 was a busy year for rescues with 18 vessels running aground or stranding on the banks.

Mr. Willis, the Master of the Lifeboat, was a perceptive man and he suggested to the Brethren that during storms and gales with lashing rain and heavy seas pounding the shore, keeping a lookout was very difficult. Mr. Willis proposed that a lookout hut, properly secure and with a bell to muster the crew when they were required for a call out would go some way to improve the lifeboat's performance. The Brethren agreed with the Master and soon a wooden hut was bolted to the ground for security and a large bell was installed, these two innovations proved very useful.

Times, were however, changing and steam tugs were emerging to claim a place in Marine history. They were certainly well received in the Humber, for a schooner the 'Rebecca and Elizabeth' of Hartlepool ran onto the Stony Binks and a steam tug from Grimsby arrived and dragged her off and towed her into Grimsby. This was the first time a steam tug had been mentioned assisting the lifeboat at Spurn, previously the lifeboat had struggled to tow refloated vessels to Hull and Grimsby.

On December 3rd and 4th a gale force wind whipped the grey waters of the Humber into a boiling turmoil, a sloop ran aground near the old cottages, but no one was found on board.

The lifeboat's log recorded the events as follows:-
"**Noon** - A perfect Hurricane; Wind, WNW; The weather very hazy. In the intervals of clear weather several vessels were running out of the Humber apparently parted or slipped from their anchors.
P.M. - Saw a large ship dismasted and a schooner full of water. Large quantities of wreck washing onto shore.
8 p.m. - Picked up 3 boats marked 'Betsy' of Blythe, 'Richard' of Ipswich and one with no name. One boat picked up by Countrymen had dead man on her.
10 p.m. - The ship that was dismasted came ashore near the sloop. Her name was 'Levant' of Frederickshaven, the sloop's name was 'Neptune' of Gravelines.

December 4th. Fore Part. Blowing Hard, N.W.
Noon - Wind more moderate.
P.M. - Wind S.W. 5 vessels to be seen on Trinity Sands, 2 of them on their broadsides, another full of water. Latter part. Fresh Breeze."

The Spurn Point Lifeboat also had its share of buffetting by the heavy seas and gales. Frequent repairs had to be undertaken, as many times the lifeboat had been thrown against the stranded ships and sustained damage. She would be towed to Hull for attention then towed back to Spurn.

Mr. Willis continued as Master of the lifeboat and Public house until September 1865 when he was appointed Keeper of the Light at Killingholme. His position was taken by Fewson Hopper who had been employed as mate and was considered as suitable for the responsible position.

The Admiralty had spent a lot of time and money on coastal defences in the Spurn area. The work seemed endless but essential. When it was completed, their Lordships issued a statement banning any removal of sand, shingle or gravel from the Spurn Peninsula.

The Brethren again tried to intercede on behalf of the lifeboat crew and it was finally agreed that the crew would dig sand and shingle at a charge of 1d per ton paid to the Board of Trade. This stipulation, however, did not last long and soon men from Kilnsea and Easington were found abusing the regulations and were digging sand and gravel from other parts of Spurn, so the Admiralty reacted angrily to this blatant breach of their regulations. They then prohibited the total excavation of any sand, gravel and shingle from the whole area, except the Binks where there was gravel for everyone, if you watched the tides!!! So once again the crew had a source of income removed, records did reveal that they did earn a little by crabbing.

Spurn Point itself was changing with the constant erosion, and a series of breaches appeared. The first was about 400 yards wide and was caused by a gale at the end of 1849, so Spurn became a series of islands at high tides. This serious situation became so bad that the Government funded work to close the breaches and the building of groynes to dissipate the force of the waves. This work was completed in 1870 with the massive chalk bank overlooking the Spurn Bight and the Greedy Gut. This bank bolstered the sea defences and the sea retreated but the threat will always remain.

The Post Office, in 1871, succeeded in providing a telegraph at Spurn and thus the Master of the Lifeboat could inform the Brethren of Hull of any stranded ships or nautical mishaps to shipping in the area. The Brethren also found the telegraph was more efficient.

Good news for the crew came in March 1873 when the Brethren decided that the lifeboat crew could have ALL the salvage money shared out, instead of allotting an eleventh part to the upkeep of the lifeboat as had happened since 1856.

The cottages built to house the crew in 1857 had been constructed to give some protection from the sea, but the constant erosion of the beaches made the buildings vulnerable to the high seas and winter gales. This state of threat made it necessary to use sand and shingle and planks to give more protection at the back of the buildings, this work cost £150.

The lifeboat was still very active, going to the assistance of vessels grounded on the sand banks and the infamous Stony Binks. One rescue is worthy of relating from the Master's Log:-

"Monday, Christmas Day, 1876, easterly heavy gale and showers of snow and sleet, heavy seas on the Binks. The lifeboat ready for probable call out. At daybreak the watch on lookout reported a vessel sunk on the Binks, the lifeboat proceeded to the wreck, but owing to the strong flood tide running over the Binks, the lifeboat was unable to make much headway against it. No.3 Pilot Cutter took us in tow and tried to tow us out but no good, so the Pilot Cutter transferred us over to the Steamer 'Swanland'. Then entering the Humber, I asked him if he would take us out to the Middle Bull buoy which he kindly did. We got under 'Canvas' and 'Shot to Windward' of the sunken vessel. When we got near the wreck it was identified as the 'Grace Darling' of Goole with three men in the rigging all in a pitiable condition, being exposed there for twelve hours. They were not able to show distress signals as the vessel sank immediately after she struck. The sea was making a clear breach over her and with considerable difficulty we succeeded in getting the men off and into the lifeboat. The Captain was so benumbed that he couldn't help himself out, so one of the lifeboat men, Edward Weldrake, went up into the rigging and got a rope around his waist and by that means we were able to get him into the lifeboat. Weldrake had to force the Captain's frozen fingers clear of the rigging, poor Weldrake had to jump from the lifeboat into the boiling sea to get to the 'Grace Darling', a very brave fellow and his reward came some 4 months later when in April 1877 the RNLI presented him with their Silver Medal and a copy of their vote inscribed on Vellum."

Being a member of the lifeboat crew at Spurn in the 19th century was a hard, tough responsible job. The luxuries of life were not to be found at Spurn. Austere conditions and accommodations, plain food, lots of fish and a limited variety of life had to suffice. A strong element of danger was always present and every time you stepped into the lifeboat one could never tell what risks would be involved. The weather was severe as all exposed regions are, so a strong physique was essential.

The isolation of the job didn't suit some of the crew and so there were many changes. In December 1877 the then Master of the Lifeboat, Fewson Hopper, was appointed lighthouse keeper at Saltend and his position was taken by the mate of the boat, Thomas Winson. The use of the smaller boat known as the tender, did not please some of the crew.

A new tender was bought by the Brethren in 1877 and a new lifeboat was acquired in 1881, being built by John Cooper for £195. The old boat had done well, being purchased in November 1854. It had saved 77 people and had assisted 97 vessels aground or wrecked.

In August 1880, Lloyds of London decided to install a signal station at Spurn and they approached the Brethren to ask for their co-operation. The Brethren, after discussion agreed to Lloyds using the lookout hut and signal mast.

The full force gales and heavy seas of December 11th 1883 caused many problems for the Master and crew of the Spurn lifeboat, for at dawn the next day the lifeboat, which had been moored instead of being safe in the boathouse, was missing. The crew couldn't believe their eyes, it was inconceivable that the lifeboat could have disappeared, but it had . . . . . The thought was now that it had broken from its mooring in the appalling weather of the previous days, but where had it gone? Perhaps it had been smashed to bits by the terrible weather conditions. Signals were sent to all shipping by various means to look out for the boat and the old retired lifeboat was 'awoken from its slumbers' and repaired as necessary. Some re-caulking was done and generally made water tight and fit for limited use. Luckily the old boat was not used a lot and on Christmas Day the missing lifeboat was found. It had been towed into Nieu Dieppe, Holland having been found by Dutch fishermen near the Island of Texel.

Mr. Matthew Brown, an Elder Brethren of Hull Trinity House, went over to Holland to arrange for the lifeboat to be brought back to Hull for repair on the steamer 'European'. The errant lifeboat was landed at Hull on January 7th 1884 and after a complete overhaul it was towed back to Spurn to resume its duties.

In 1888, the small lifeboat tender was torn from its moorings by a severe gale and blown out to sea. It was eventually found in a parlous condition near Yarmouth, the damage was so severe that it was adjudged to be beyond economical repair. The Brethren decided to replace it and gave Messrs. Emery, Boat Builders of Sheringham in Norfolk, an order to supply a new boat measuring 21ft by 7ft 6 inch beam for the sum of £21.

In July 1888, the Master of the Lifeboat sent a report to the Brethren stating that the crew were often called out at night to go the assistance of vessels showing red lights, firing flares and distress rockets. After several of these calls, which proved to be false alarms and the sport of the crews of fishing vessels, the lifeboat crews didn't see the joke and objected that they could not attend genuine distress calls if they were being summoned to bogus alarms for the amusement of fishing vessels wasting their time. The Brethren took a very serious view of the affair and wrote to the fishing companies and all other companies sending ships to sea telling them of the events and warning everyone to stop this mischievous practice.

Records of 1890 reveal that since February 1882, a period of 8 years, the Spurn lifeboat had given assistance to 49 vessels requiring assistance and had taken ashore 224 people. In some cases, if a vessel refloated, then the crew would re-board the ship and continue their voyage, but in other cases the vessels became total wrecks on the infamous sands. The total salvage awards to the Spurn lifeboat to that date amounted to £813-8-8d.

The crew's concern for their children's education became paramount in 1890 when the Master wrote to the Brethren on the subject. They set the wheels in motion and in October of that year a school building was in the course of erection by W. Lison, a Hull Builder. This building was to cost £170 and would offer a much needed facility for the children of Spurn.

The building was sparse but functional, being a one roomed rectangular brick edifice. It measured 26ft by 20ft with a door in the west wall, two windows in each of the other three walls and it would be heated by a coke stove in the middle of the room. The school was opened for use in January 1891 and twenty children attended. However, it must be remembered that the school was first and foremost for the children of the lifeboat crew, the other children came from the other areas of Spurn.

In 1893 the Brethren applied to the Education Authority at Kilnsea for a certified teacher. The school attained elementary status under the Education Authority, the Brethren paying a £10 premium per annum. By now the school was declared open to ALL children in the area including the children of the Lighthouse Keepers.

The Archbishop of York paid a visit to Spurn on June 13th 1893 when he was travelling down the Humber in the Trinity House Yacht. He landed by small boat at Spurn Point and a Service was held in the school room, then the Primate and his party walked the $3\frac{1}{2}$ miles to Kilnsea where they were conveyed by horse drawn vehicles to Patrington Vicarage where they enjoyed the hospitality of the local Vicar for the night. The result of this visit was that a Service was to be held every Sunday at Spurn.

Lifeboatmen's houses and Smeaton's lighthouse with the other seaward lighthouse and its pier.
The 'Lifeboat Inn' can be seen in the background. c.1891.
Welholme Galleries, Grimsby.

A telephone had been installed in the Master's house with lines to the Coastguard Stations at Easington and Kilnsea for immediate communication if a vessel needed assistance.

The Master of the Lifeboat, Mr. Thomas Winson, retired in 1894 and David Pye was appointed to the position at a wage of £80 per year, the mate was paid £52 per year and the crew received 13/- per week. All salvage money was shared among the Master, the mate and the crew in proportion and the crew were expected to pay a nominal rent of 1/- a month for their cottage. The upkeep of the station was at that time costing Hull Trinity House over £400 per year.

In the year 1895, 4 ships ran aground in the area of Spurn Point but all of them were able to refloat without the assistance of the lifeboat. However, in 1896, 9 vessels ran on the gravel banks of the Stony Binks and the treacherous Trinity sands, and 3 of them needed the aid of the Spurn lifeboat.

In 1897, the RNLI, after long discussions with Hull Trinity House, decided to station the steam lifeboat 'James Stevens No.3' in Grimsby's Dock Basin. She was certainly big and powerful but the disadvantages were her appetite for coal and inevitable delays in raising steam thus reducing the lifeboat's availability. She really was on evaluation trials and did not reach the peak of reliability or performance during her $4\frac{1}{2}$ years at Grimsby. In 1903 she was sent to Gorleston for further trials but she never returned to Grimsby.

In the Master's report of 1898, he revealed that most of the vessels stranded on the Binks or Trinity sands were being refloated with the assistance of tugs from either Grimsby or Hull.

Before the advent of steam tugs, refloating a grounded ship was sometimes attempted by 'Carrying out an Anchor'. This meant going alongside the stranded vessel and taking her anchor and dropping it in, hopefully, deeper water where it would bite into the sea bed and grip, then the stranded ship would use the purchase to haul herself off the bank. This method was, in most cases, extremely dangerous and was certainly not part of the lifeboat's accepted duties and was frowned upon by the Brethren. As previously stated, a lifeboat saves lives not ships.

In 1901, the Spurn lifeboat was suffering from wear and tear. The constant battering and much use had taken their toll and extensive repairs were necessary. Luckily the RNLI in Grimsby were able to offer the Spurn Station the loan of the old 'Manchester Unity' as Grimsby had the steam lifeboat 'James Stevens No.3'.

This arrangement would take care of the period of time when the Spurn boat was at Hull being overhauled. However, when the Spurn boat was examined at Hull prior to repair, it was found to be beyond economical repair and the Brethren decided to order a new lifeboat. This time the order was given to Messrs. Earles of Hull who submitted to most favourable price. She was to cost £700 and her measurements would be 34ft 6 inches long by 9ft 10 inches beam, she would have 2 masts with sails and would row 10 oars. This new boat was delivered to Spurn Point on January 3rd 1903.

The experiment of the Steam Lifeboat at Grimsby's Royal Dock Basin was not a success for reasons of availability and the RNLI considered transferring the steam boat to Spurn and providing a permanent mooring. The Brethren and the RNLI considered the options very carefully, but in the end realised the attendant problems of fuel, supplies, servicing, etc., meant that the idea was not feasible and so it was dismissed.

The Spurn lifeboat continued its good work under the management of the Brethren of Hull Trinity House until January 1st 1908 when the Humber Conservancy Board constituted by the Humber Conservancy Act of 1907, took over the Station.

So ended 97 years of operation through difficulties and triumphs, carried out with the backing and support of the Hull Trinity House. This long suffering establishment had paid out considerable sums of money to keep the Station going and without their help lifeboats certainly would not have lasted long at Spurn Point. The assistance given to ships in the most atrocious weather conditions cannot be forgotten. The early lifeboats were difficult to handle and were primitive in the extreme although up to date at the time. The courage of the lifeboat crews was beyond description, they never gave a thought for their own safety and earned the overwhelming gratitude of the fortunate survivors who were plucked from the jaws of death by these brave men.

The Humber Conservancy Board looked after the operation of the lifeboat station in the interim period for 3 years when the RNLI took over in 1911.

Crew and lifeboat of the Hull Trinity House at Spurn, probably at the turn of the century.
Town Docks Museum, Hull.

CHAPTER THREE

METAMORPHOSIS 1908-1911

The period of time between 1908 and 1911 was to prove significant to the Coxswain and crew of the Spurn Point lifeboat service, as from January 1908 the responsbility of the manning, maintenance and establishment of the lifeboat operation now rested with the newly formed Humber Conservancy Board and they did not want to know at all. After all this liability had been thrown into their lap and they felt, perhaps quite rightly, that the obvious body suitable to operate a lifeboat establishment was the RNLI, but there was a sting in the tail and that was that the Coxswain and crew were all full time and had to be paid as such.

Time would reveal that the RNLI and the HCB would do all they could to avoid grasping this particular nettle. Correspondence flowed between them, argument followed argument, offers were made, threats, thinly disguised, were uttered but if it hadn't been for the Board of Trade in London, who intervened to sort out the sordid mess, it is very possible that the lifeboat at Spurn Point would have been abandoned in 1908, such was the perilous situation.

Imagine the HCB's horror when they found out that this liability had strings attached to it. The Lifeboat Coxswain and crew wanted paying as full time staff, quite unheard of in those Edwardian days. Very quickly the HCB issued a report to the other members of the HCB stating that they regarded the lifeboat operation as not necessary and the HCB thought a 'Philanthropic object' and certainly not a paying proposition. To give this august body credit, while they were arguing with all and sundry, they did very reluctantly pay the Cox and crew.

When the HCB studied the finances of the lifeboat establishment they received another shock as the outlay on average totalled £480 and the receipts from rents came to £18-9-0.

The HCB thought about the unwelcome situation. The Chairman Mr. W. S. Wright and his committee debated and argued among themselves, having been thrown the problem who would take it off their hands?

A letter from David Pye, the Coxswain of the Spurn lifeboat, to Alfred Franklin, the secretary to the Board of the HCB, drew attention to the crews request for a pay increase. Trinity House had always been sympathetic to the crews problems and had tried to offer help in every way and Mr. Pye thought that HCB might feel favourable obliged to his request. It was like waving a red flag at a bull. Records do not tell us how the HCB reacted but the plight of the crew was indeed desperate. Pye's letter pointed out that the gravel deposits had thinned out considerably and in another letter dated March 3rd, the Coxswain pointed out in detail the various sources of income, such as crabbing, fishing, gravelling, etc., the total sum of these money making efforts was under £53 to be shared out among 9 men. Pye emphasised that there was no other means of extra money to be earned, also the cost of twine for rigging up the crab gear and the cost of upkeep of the boats had to be taken into account.

In a reply to a letter from Mr. A. M. Jackson of Andrew M. Jackson (Solicitors) who represented the Humber Conservancy Board, Mr. Pye stated that on March 23rd 1908 there were 13 families living at Spurn, 10 families living in the 10 cottages numbering 56, 2 families were at the lighthouse numbering 9, and at the Lifeboat Inn 9 people resided. The schoolmaster lived as a lodger at one of the lifeboat cottages, there were no resident Coastguards, the nearest Coastguard Station was at Easington. Their signal station was at Spurn and stood on Trinity House land and had just been enlarged. The Lloyds signal station also stood on Trinity House land, there were no other buildings except in connection with the lifeboat cottages, viz, the lifeboat watch house and boathouse and some small sheds to store essential gear, total numbers of inhabitants 75.

The HCB were from the start determined to leave no

stone unturned to prove their case for disestablishing the lifeboat station at Spurn and the reasons were given again, that the HCB regarded the maintenance of a lifeboat and the payment of the crew as 'entirely a philanthropic matter'. A letter from Alfred Franklin, secretary to the HCB, to Messrs. Stamp, Jackson and Birks Solicitors, stated that a report was being prepared which would set out the reasons for the HCB's desire to give up all obligations and interests at Spurn Point as they saw the RNLI as the obvious body to operate and maintain the Lifeboat Station. This letter was sent to the aforementioned Solicitors for their perusal and advice, records do not show their reply or advice.

A letter on 27th March 1908, from Trinity House to Andrew M. Jackson, solicitors, to the HCB stating the origins of the lifeboat operation at Spurn and Mr. Francis Constable's part in the scheme, stressing that Trinity House only managed the lifeboat service in the interests of the preservation of lives of seagoing folk. The involvement of Trinity House was purely voluntary and not mandatory or statutory.

In the strenuous campaign conducted by the HCB in the 3 years, the arguments between them and the RNLI became acrimonious and bitter, and was a very unsettling influence on the operation of the lifeboat service.

Mr. Franklin stated in a letter dated 10th April 1908 to Commander W. S. Atkin who was the Marine Superintendent of the Lancashire and Yorkshire Railway Company based at Goole, that he had a conversation with Alderman Massey about Spurn and its lifeboat problem and the letter informed him that sundry documents and agreements were available which he contended that Trinity House were bound to keep and maintain a lifeboat at Spurn. Mr. Massey's impression was that there was some arrangement between the Hull Trinity House and the London Trinity House that provided for this arrangement.

A letter from Mr. Franklin of the HCB to the secretary of the RNLI in London dated 18th May 1908, informed that he has been instructed by the HCB to report on the subject of Spurn Point and the lifeboat facility. After much discussion the above mentioned resolved 'that the RNLI be asked whether they are prepared to take over the management of the lifeboat at Spurn, and if so on what terms?'

Again the HCB laboured their opinion that, however deserving, the HCB was a commercial body and not a philanthropic society and it scarcely fell into their province to maintain this lifeboat and its operation.

An invitation to the RNLI for a visit to Spurn to inspect the Lifeboat Station and facilities was offered to the Officials of the RNLI and a steam launch was available to convey any RNLI Official(s) was also extended.

Mr. C. Dibdin, secretary of the RNLI, replied to this letter on 19th May stating that the HCB invitation would be considered by the Committee of Management at the next meeting which would be on June 4th 1908.

A letter dated 4th June from Mr. Dibdin of RNLI to Mr. Franklin HCB, accepting the invitation for a visit to Spurn by senior officials of the RNLI and the senior members of the HCB Board, the RNLI would send Commander C. E. Cunninghame-Graham, MVO, RN.

Next to enter the scene was Commander W. S. Atkin RN who was also travelling to Spurn with the other high powered officials on the HCB Yacht 'Queen'. This Gentleman was the Marine Superintendent of the Lancashire and Yorkshire Railway Company and was based in Goole. He was also Chairman of the Marine and Works Committee of the HCB and was a firm friend and confident of Mr. W. S. Wright, the Chairman of the HCB.

Commander Cunninghame-Graham wrote to Mr. Franklin on 14th June to say how he was looking forward to the sea trip to Spurn and that he would be bringing his Deputy Captain, Thomas Holmes, along for the ride. Franklin wrote back to inform the writer of the arrangements for the 25th June, the Conversancy yacht 'Queen' would leave Victoria Pier Hull at 10.30am on 7th July.

A late hiccup from the HCB when they discovered a spare lifeboat in Hull and decided to ask Cunninghame-Graham to inspect it when he visited Hull to embark on the yacht. A time was arranged for 9.30am. The Coxswain of the Spurn lifeboat Mr. D. Pye was prevailed on by Franklin for details of how many occasions the lifeboat crew had been called out over the last 10 years and could these services have been performed without the need of a lifeboat?

Letters of the same nature went to Trinity House, one wonders if trust wasn't very evident in those days.

RNLI were now pressing HCB for the details from Pye. One imagines he was busy saving lives at sea, although the records still do not show any evidence of the lifeboat being called out.

Commander Cunninghame-Graham was now getting impatient and was demanding to know why the details hadn't reached his desk. Franklin was flapping about in a panic, and feared Mr. Wright might summon him to his presence for a 'CHAT'. Pye still didn't hurry. Franklin wrote a grovelling letter to Cunninghame-Graham promising results. Eventually, Pye came up with the figures and they were sent hurriedly off to RNLI. The details were comprehensive and gave an accurate presentation of the situation at Spurn, both past and present.

A letter from Charles Dibdin RNLI, informing HCB of their decision not to take over the lifeboat establishment at Spurn, did more to alarm the marine and works committee than they could imagine. A lot of midnight oil was burned in discussion and scurrying around with messages for Messrs. Wright and Atkin, who were not in the least pleased. If anything, it served to harden their determination to get rid of the lifeboat and its liabilities.

At last on 10th December 1908, a letter from the RNLI landed on Franklin's desk. He opened it with some trepidation. The reply was bland, but it was what Franklin had expected. The RNLI would NOT be interested in paying the full time crew, there was no further comment. Franklin sent off an acknowledgement and put the RNLI letter on the agenda for the next Board meeting when it would be dissected in great detail.

Franklin, of course informed Mr. W. S. Wright and Commander Atkin of the contents of the RNLI's letter. Their reaction was very predictable, fury was a better description.

On Mr. Wright's instruction, Franklin wrote again to the RNLI on December 14th 1908 to enquire, tongue in cheek, whether the RNLI proposed, if they would eventually take over the running of the Spurn station, to pay the crew for launches and practices, and perhaps the RNLI would consider this point and clarify it.

On December 15th Charles Dibdin of the RNLI London wrote back to Franklin stating what his Committee should have done earlier and what the HCB feared. They certainly did not intend to pay the crew of the lifeboat for launches or practice and in order to rub this point in Mr. Dibdin underlined that they intended to stick rigidly to their original terms and conditions mentioned in the reply to the HCB's first letter.

On December 19th 1908, Franklin wrote to David Pye at Spurn and proceeded to lay the law down to the unfortunate Coxswain, stating that whereas in the past the Cox and crew of the lifeboat had negotiated for salvage due to the crew for successful rescues, from now on the marine and works committee under the chairmanship of Commander Atkin would be taking this matter in hand.

David Pye was therefore directed to report all occasions on which assistance was rendered by the lifeboat and he was reminded that under no circumstances must he or his crew enter into any agreements or any other transactions.

Franklin wanted an acknowledgement of this letter by return. At the next HCB board meeting, the committee discussed the RNLI's reply to Franklin's letter with disappointment. HCB were still lumbered with the confounded lifeboat and its crew. Franklin was again instructed to write back to Dibdin and grovel to see if anything could be salvaged, also a threat could be introduced that the HCB now was considering the total abandonment of the lifeboat operation.

To Franklin's surprise, the reply from Dibdin was courteous and formal but did not mention the HCB proposal to abandon the lifeboat operation.

So ended 1908, a year of uncertainty and wrangling, especially for the Cox and crew at Spurn. They didn't know what was going on. The only link was with Pye and Franklin and relations between them were rather strained. The constant battle between the HCB and the

RNLI was disgraceful if one considers these two wealthy bodies, both of which could well afford to pay the unfortunate men at Spurn. All the unpleasantness and bickering could have been avoided to reach a solution at any time.

Research, however, does not reveal any details of life at Spurn during 1908 nor any accounts of the launching of the lifeboat for assistance. We do know, however, that the HCB reluctantly continued to pay the lifeboat crew, at the old rate. No pay increase had resulted from the crew's request, so they had to supplement their earnings with fishing, crabbing, and digging the rapidly dwindling gravel.

The HCB policy was to rid themselves of this burden to anyone who showed the remotest interest. Unfortunately there were not many of these potential bodies about, mainly because of the financial involvement with the payments to the Cox and his crew. For better or worse this precedent of the full time crew stemmed from the days of the lifeboat's inception when the Hull Trinity House administered the service. In those days a full time crew worked very well and so the problems of the ballast and cobbles thinning out did not occur. Who could have foreseen that in later years these men would be on the bread line because of lack of potential work and hardly a living wage.

All the wrangling and bitter arguments between the HCB and the RNLI left one point that all sides seemed to have missed and that was the position of the men at Spurn. As previously discussed above, the crew were living on a bare subsistence. These gallant men, the very people that Mr. Wright and his friends wanted to get rid of so badly, the lifeboat crew, who went out to rescues in the most appalling weather conditions to rescue the unlucky folk that went down to the sea in ships and became stranded.

We know that the finances of the HCB and the RNLI were more than adequate to pay the Coxswain and his crew a good wage commensurate with the value of the arduous, dangerous task of saving lives at sea. In fact both sides at one time or another made the point that their refusal to take over the lifeboat operation was due to a matter of principle. How incredible to talk about principles!!!

Mention is made of the offer of the RNLI to operate the lifeboat establishment and contribute £150 towards the maintenance, but the HCB refused to accept this gesture of goodwill as realistic. The HCB still saw the RNLI as the most appropriate body to handle this entity, in turn the RNLI saw the picture somewhat differently. They saw a monolithic board set up by the Parliament to handle most objects in the River Humber and its environs, wielding great powers, administered by captains of industry whose integrity was supposed to be par excellence, behaving like a spoilt child who couldn't have its own way.

One must feel very grateful that the Board of Trade stepped in and at least tried to act as honest broker.

Even the efforts of the Board of Trade were not wanted by the protagonists. The HCB wanted to abandon and disestablish the whole lifeboat operation as soon as possible. The RNLI sent some high powered officials in the HCB yacht 'Queen' to Spurn to see the sights but again nothing came of this venture.

The accommodation at Spurn Point comprised 10 cottages built about 1858 by public subscription on ground granted by the late Mr. Francis Constable. At a later date, Hull Trinity House took a succession of 21 year leases of the land but the last of these lapsed and the HCB were year to year tenants, this tenancy could be terminated by HCH on a 6 month notice.

In the year 1909 it was disclosed that the lifeboat had been launched on average 6 times a year and in the last 7 years, 31 lives had been saved, 26 vessels were assisted and one vessel sank. It was understood that recently very few services had been rendered to vessels bound to or from the Humber estuary, an incredible statement if one considers the steady growth of the fishing industry both in Hull and Grimsby. The increase in commercial trade bringing shipping in far greater numbers into the River Humber, so can we believe the previous statement or was it to discredit the lifeboat service?

In an attempt to wriggle off the hook, the HCB tried to arrange a meeting with the officials of the RNLI in

London. The HCB delegation comprised of Mr. W. W. Wright, Chairman HCB, Commander W. S. Atkin of the Lancashire and Yorkshire Railway and Chairman of the Marine and Works Committee of the HCB based at Goole, and the Secretary, Mr. Alfred Franklin, who went along to take the notes.

Mr. Franklin was instructed to write to Charles Dibdin, Secretary of the RNLI, and arrange a date for such a meeting. In response to Franklin's, Dibdin wrote back to offer May 25th at 11.30am. This was subsequently altered to 3pm.

It would now appear that Wright and Atkin were going to try to pressurise the RNLI into taking over the Spurn station by threatening to abandon the establishment altogether, although no mention was made about this ploy before the meeting in London.

A letter dated 17th June 1909 from Charles Dibdin of the RNLI gave some details of the meeting between RNLI and HCB, the information was as expected. Both sides laid down their ideas and limits. It seemed that the vexed problem of the Spurn lifeboat station was discussed in very great detail but as both sides were absolutely intransigent, no acceptable conclusion was reached and the two protagonists retired to lick their wounds and reflect on whether the meeting was a waste of time and effort.

The only tangible thing to give cause for thought was the offer of the RNLI of £150 per annum to go towards the upkeep and maintenance of the lifeboat operation.

At a meeting of the HCH, it was resolved that Franklin should write to the RNLI and tell them that regretfully the HCB could not accept any of the proposals placed on the table at the meeting in London by the RNLI. In fact the proposals did not break any new ground at all, and the Chairman, Mr. Wright, declared that in future the agenda must be consulted before any further exchange of ideas, and he emphasised this point so as to save going over the same old arguments again.

Franklin refers to a letter from a Mr. Newell, a member of the HCB Board, received on September 6th last. The contents of Mr. Newell's letter covered his wish that Franklin should provide all needfall data re Spurn lifeboat establishment prior to his proposal that the HCB should make every move to abandon this onerous responsibility.

It would appear that the HCB's patience was wearing thin by now because it was now very apparent that the majority of the members of the HCB Board were of the same mind, and that mood was ominously anti-lifeboat station.

A letter was sent to the RNLI by Franklin on September 13th 1909 containing a statement in the following form:-

"That having regard to the fact that negotiations with RNLI relative to their taking over the lifeboat at Spurn have not resulted in the RNLI making any proposal which meets with the approval of the HCB, steps be taken to terminate the tenancy of the cottages and dispense with the services of the lifeboat and crew with the object of disestablishing the lifeboat station at the "EARLIEST POSSIBLE DATE".

However, on 15th September 1909, a letter from William Spicer, assistance secretary, RNLI London, refers to previous correspondence and comments on the present state of affairs which existed between the RNLI and the HCB. Mr. Spicer thought that the position of the RNLI in this matter had not been made totally clear to the HCB, the difficulty encountered by the RNLI was not a financial one but a one of principle. (Mr. Wright had hinted that he thought otherwise). The RNLI were unable to take over the establishment at Spurn not because it would become too costly but because it would involve them in responsibilities which were outside their function. To take over the lifeboat establishment and to pay a permanent crew for which they could not find any other occupation except on the occasion of a ship in distress would be in their opinion, ULTRA VIRES. Mr. Spicer went on to state that this difficulty did not affect the HCB as the onus was already resting with the HCB. Nevertheless, the RNLI had been desirous of meeting the views of the HCB and had made an offer of £150 per annum which, according to the information before them, seemed reasonable."

Meanwhile, the writer expressed the hope that the

HCB would refrain from taking ay immediate action in disestablishing the Lifeboat Station.

This inflamatory letter was shown by Franklin to Andrew Jackson, the HCB Solicitor for his perusal. After a day or two his reply reached Franklin, Mr. Jackson's views were that RNLI should come up with counter proposals not HCB. RNLI's point about having no powers to pay full time lifeboat crew not accepted. Mr. Jackson thought that the RNLI as a voluntary institution were sufficiently elastic for this situation to allow, and although the appointment of a full time permanent crew would be an exception, the circumstances were certainly exceptional too.

Letter from Mr. W. S. Wright to William Spicer, assistant secretary RNLI, dated 18th September 1909. Mr. Wright was anxious to emphasise that his colleagues on the HCB Board were fully aware of the current situation and he was angry that aspirations were hinted at that he did not give his Board the full details of the matter in discussion.

Mr. Wright repeated the information that at their last meeting on September 9th the members of the HCB Board resolved that it was their intention to abolish the lifeboat establishment at Spurn on the following grounds:-

1. That it was entirely in their option to maintain it or abolish it.

2. That unless there was a commensurate advantage to them as a Conservancy Board, it was a needlessly heavy burden on their funds.

3. That statistics of services rendered tend to show that the need of it was less conspicuous than formerly shown.

4. These statistics applied less to vessels navigating the Humber or trading to Humber Ports than to coasting vessels of a comparatively small size or craft bound from or to other ports, from which they of course derived no revenue.

5. That if it was nevertheless contended that a lifeboat should continue to be stationed at Spurn or at any equally more suitable spot in the vicinity, the RNLI, constituted as it was with its vast and continually reinforced resources and special equipment for that purpose, it was the proper body to take this matter in hand and in such matters as they deemed right and in accordance with their powers.

Mr. Wright stressed that it was not his or the HCB's intention to enter into a protracted argument or slanging match, but he thought that it was enough to remind the RNLI that the object of the HCB in communicating with the RNLI in this matter was mainly to guard against the possibility that the HCB might be reproached for any ommissions, to do so after the event if they should decide to abandon the lifeboat station would not be in anybody's interests so that explained the painstaking statement of the current set of circumstances, the proposal the RNLI have made (£150 per annum) did not satisfy the opinions of the HCB Board and therefore the HCB has exercised its freedom of action and had resolved to abandon the lifeboat establishment at Spurn Point.

Details of the lifeboats activities in 1909 supplied by the Coxswain at Spurn, Mr. David Pye:-

March 23rd. SS 'Nidaros' of Esbjerg, outward bound from Grimsby stranded on Spurn Point, proceeded in lifeboat tender (small boat equipped for such assistance), stood by vessel until she refloated on next tide.

October 31st. 1909. Bull lightship drifting up river after being in collision with vessel 'Orinoco' crew of lifeboat assisted with lowering lightship anchors to secure her.

December 22nd 1909. SS 'John' bound for Middlesbrough with cargo of chemical salts stranded off Dimlington, 8 lives saved by lifeboat, vessel sank.

Not many call outs but the lifeboat was there if needed as with all rescue services. These figures would be heaven sent to the hard line men on the HCB Board, what capital they could make to prove their case. "It never gets called out, it isn't necessary. Why spend hundreds of pounds for a service that is hardly used? Let's abolish the whole operation, nobody needs it."

However, on October 7th 1909, Mr. Wright had a letter from Mr. Thomas Pelham of the Board of Trade in London, who was most concerned by reports of the HCB's peremptory decision to abolish the Spurn lifeboat. Mr. Pelham understood that there had been difficulties and differences of opinion with the RNLI but wished to offer the services of the Board of Trade to find a way out of this problem. Mr. Pelham requested Mr. Wright to advise him of the present situation so that communication could be established between the interested parties.

Mr. Wright replied with the HCB's side of the argument.

Franklin wrote to Commander Atkin and told him about Pelham's letter to Wright, he even sent Atkin a copy of the letter on 23rd October 1909. Atkin wrote back telling Franklin to keep quiet about the Board of Trade's letter for the time being and he, Atkin, was still convinced that the lifeboat service should be abolished as soon as possible and he would of course back the chairman in this matter.

A telegram arrived at Franklin's office on November 19th 1909. It was from Mr. Pelham, BOT, asking Franklin to arrange a meeting at the BOT's Office in London as soon as possible. A date was mentioned, November 21st, and Franklin wrote to Atkin and told him of Pelham's suggestion for a meeting and a date. Atkin wanted a talk with Wright before the meeting, he feared that Pelham would become too persuasive and talk them into changing their minds if they were not very well prepared. Franklin was to accompany the two officials to add weight to the case.

Notes made by Franklin tell the old old story. The near threadbare arguments and the now familiar threat to abolish the lifeboat station, lock, stock and barrel, also an incredible statement issued from these two captains of industry. They actually implied that the lifeboat station could be disestablished without subjecting anyone to inconvenience or interference with navigation in the Humber or the work of Lloyds signal station at Spurn. What a bald statement of arrant nonsense.

A letter from Mr. Pelham of the Board of Trade Lodon, suggesting that the HCB should never even consider abandoning the lifeboat station which had been in existence for over 100 years and had a fine record of saving lives and assisting vessels in distress in or around the Spurn Peninsula. Mr. Pelham went on to say that had the possibility of contemplated closure been formed by Act of Parliament, a clause might have been inserted into the Act to preclude such an action to close the lifeboat station!

Mr. Pelham noted the offer of the RNLI to offer the sum of £150 per annum as a contribution to the maintenance of the establishment and the BOT would, in the interests of keeping the lifeboat station extant, be prepared to offer the sum of £100 per annum towards the cost of upkeep at Spurn. Mr. Pelham expressed regret that he had heard from the RNLI that very morning to say that they did not wish to discuss with the HCB the question of the lifeboat station.

In spite of the efforts made by Mr. Pelham and his colleagues at the Board of Trade, the chairman of the HCB would not agree to his proposals and intimated that the decision made by the HCB Board to abolish the lifeboat station stood and would be implemented as soon as possible.

A further letter from Mr. Pelham to Mr. W. S. Wright on December 9th, asked Mr. Wright to reconsider the HCB's decision and Mr. Pelham went on to say that a letter concerning the lifeboat question would be sent to Franklin very soon and again he hoped that no action would be effected concerning the abolition of the lifeboat station.

A letter from RNLI to Franklin HCB on December 9th concerning service acetylene beach lights which had proved a great assistance in the launching of lifeboats at night. However, a case had arisen of a light vessel keeper mistaking the beach light for a vessel in distress causing him to take appropriate action in the case of an emergency. RNLI wrote to inform HCB that one of these lights had been placed at Mablethorpe Lifeboat Station and should any other of these lights be furnished by the RNLI at lifeboat stations in which the HCB had an interest, the Commissioners of the RNLI would inform them in good time.

"Perhaps the HCB will have the kindness, on your representation to give such instructions, as they may prevent the needless launching of lifeboats owing to the placing of the acetylene light or lights in question at stations on such points of the coast as may be connected with the Humber Conservancy Board".

We saw further diabolical moves to further the desires of Mr. W. S. Wright and his colleague Commander W. S. Atkin in 1910, but just give a thought to the crew at Spurn, this lonely isolated peninsula, subject to the extremes of weather and climate. The tough, kindly men who manned the lifeboat whose only desire was to rescue the unfortunate men and women from a ship in difficulties, who had no part in the machinations of the HCB's board. They were powerless to do anything other than sit tight and man the lifeboat when necessary. Their time would come again to prove their value to a more appreciative body of men, but first of all the current situation had to be resolved with the goodwill of the Board of Trade in London.

It would appear that the Humber Conservancy Board's suspicious attitude to all suggestions from all quarters continued to make life difficult for the lifeboat station at Spurn during 1910.

Correspondence relating to the RNLI beach lights continued into January and on the 14th day of the month Mr. Franklin wrote to the RNLI to inform them that the RNLI would be required to be given good notice when beach lights were to be positioned at lifeboat stations governed by the HCB. Mr. Franklin also maintained that he regarded the lights as a hazard to lifeboats and other shipping.

A letter from the Board of Trade in London to Mr. Franklin, stating their concern about the HCB's determination to abolish the Spurn Lifeboat Station. Mr. Pelham stated that the HCB had acted outside the confines of the Conservancy Act which was not clearly defined to cover the eventuality of closures or abandonment of the lifeboat operation, also the Board of Trade relied on communication with the lifeboat watchman to operate its rocket life saving apparatus at Easington, and to some extent depended on notice of wrecks received from the same watchman.

The Board of Trade went on to state that when the Humber Conservancy Act of 1907 was passed through Parliament under which Inter Alia, the lifeboat and station at Spurn as well as the buoyage and beaconage dues (out of which the station was maintained), were transferred from Hull Trinity House, the Board of Trade did not expect or anticipate that the Spurn lifeboat establishment would ever be considered for closure.

A letter from Mr. Franklin to Mr. W. S. Wright, the HCB chairman, enclosed Pelham's letter. Mr. Franklin had sent Commander Atkin a copy and had conversed on the subject, Franklin didn't think it wise to put Pelham's letter on the agenda for the next meeting.

A letter from Franklin to the HCB chief engineer at the HCB asked him if he would give David Pye, Cox at Spurn, details of the likely areas where the RNLI beachlights could be positioned.

A letter from Commander Atkin to Mr. Franklin dated January 14th, refering to the letter from the Board of Trade. In Atkin's opinion, the contents of this letter were far too important to be discussed by the HCB committee at such short notice. Commander Atkin proposed to write to the chairman to acquaint him with the details and a copy of the letter would be sent to Mr. Franklin.

It was very clear that both Atkin and Wright were still intent on abandoning the lifeboat establishment at Spurn at all costs. They were using the faithful Franklin as an intermediary and a buffer to absorb the howls of protest and complaints that were being received from the RNLI and the Board of Trade.

In spite of all the pleas and entreaties from all interested parties it would appear that Messrs. Atkin and Wright were deaf to common sense and reasoned thinking. The awful thoughts of shipwreck and potential loss of life because of the lifeboat facility not being available did not seem to figure in their closed minds. It was patently obvious that these two men were not capable of administering this kind of organisation especially where lives were at risk, autocracy at its worst.

Indeed, during the entire period of their tenure of the Spurn Lifeboat Station, the only thought which occurred with monotonous regularity to these two pillars of the establishment was how and when could we rid ourselves of this unnecessary burden.

In fact one wonders why these two gentlemen were considered for the positions of such responsibility. Certainly their experiences as businessmen would have been impressive but time would reveal a very unsatisfactory side of their methods.

Mr. W. S. Wright, a wealthy business man, (who, among other committments, was chairman of the Hull and Barnsley Railway) was chosen as Chairman of the Humber Conservancy Board, again his record of managing people and business must have weighed heavily in his favour. Commander W. S. Atkin, Marine Superintendent of the Lancashire and Yorkshire Railway and based at Goole must have satisfied the Government Authorities who appointed the official. All the more reason for the surprise and astonishment at some of their decisions, especially those concerning the apparent lack of regard for the safety and the future of the Spurn Lifeboat Station.

Mr. Alfred Franklin, a willing, efficient Clerk to the Board, did as he was told and as he valued his job he made sure that he informed and spied on all that would have rocked the autocratic boat. As Franklin feared for his job if he disagreed or showed disapproval at some of the more outrageous decisions made by Atkins and Wright, he instilled the same kind of respect into David Pye, the Coxswain at Spurn, who was regarded as a timid, subject. "Do as you are told, don't ask questions and you'll be alright" Franklin told him.

At this moment in time, the BOT with their very efficient clerk Mr. T. Pelham foremost in the difficult negotiations involved dealing with the HCB, tried to arrange as many meetings with the recalcitrant HCB, who made any attempt at negotiating extremely arduous and fractious. Pelham realised the potential danger to shipping in the Humber estuary without the availability of the lifeboat operation and he could not understand the hard line attitude of the officials of the HCB. It seemed to Pelham that whatever suggestion was put to Wright and Atkin, the answer was always the same. "The RNLI should take it over, its nothing to do with us, why should we bother?"

Meetings were held at great length, hope was expressed that some agreement might be found to continue the operating of the Spurn Lifeboat but the usual result was a shaking of heads and a determination to reject all Pelham's entreaties. During the next few days correspondence would ensue, and largely negative officials saying again the old response, "Why should we support the lifeboat establishment? Its got nothing to do with us. Why can't the RNLI take it over, it's not our function" or words to that effect.

Lesser men than Thomas Pelham would have given up the unequal struggle long ago but this public spirited man was determined to make something of the situation.

A letter from Thomas Pelham on 5th March 1910 asked for particulars as to the number of times the Spurn Lifeboat had been called out in the last ten years, identifying each year and also the cases relating to vessels entering or leaving the Humber estuary.

Letter from Franklin to David Pye at Spurn asked for the above mentioned details as soon as possible.

Letters from Stamp, Jackson and Birks, Solicitors acting for the Constable Settled Estates (who owned the land at Spurn). The letter dated 23rd May 1910, regarding the leases at Spurn for lifeboat cottages, etc. In 1906 the Solicitor acting for Hull Trinity House informed Stamp, Jackson and Birks that the leases held by them had run out and the Solicitor was having copies made as drafts for the new leases, but as pointed out the leases had long since run out and no notice of intention to renew had been given to Hull Trinity House.

They had no power to instruct their legal advisers to prepare new draft leases and any proposal such as those in the old agreements would have to have the sanction of the Court even if our client agreed to them, which we doubted."

Interviews between the Constable Settled Estates and the Solicitor to Hull Trinity House took place and the former agreed that Hull Trinity House should become tenants on a yearly basis, terminable by 6 months notice and under the terms of the old leases, so far as they applied from year to year.

The Trinity House Solicitor promised in a report on the matter with a request for a renewal of the leases to submit to Major W. G. R. Chichester-Constable, the present tenant for life of the Constable Settled Estates. However, Constable Estates were never informed and shortly afterwards the Humber Conservancy Bill was moved through Parliament creating The Humber Conservancy Board and empowering it to take over certain things from Hull Trinity House, along with the tenancies of the land at Spurn so we understand that HCB was now the tenant. It seems incredible that Hull Trinity House would allow the leases to lapse, was this deliberate?

In 1904 Lloyds of London and the Admiralty approached Constable Settled Estates with a view to leasing certain lands at Spurn for signalling stations and Coastguard houses. Considerable trouble was taken and series of plots were chosen and surveyed, terms were submitted to Lloyds and the Admiralty which were refused.

"It is at this stage that we must say that Constable Settle Estates had grounds for complaint. No counter proposals were made by Lloyds or the Admiralty, and quite by chance, we find that these two wealthy bodies had been allowed to take land originally leased to Hull Trinity House at a nominal rent for life saving purposes. It is this to which our client strongly objects to a certainly will not allow in future, added to which there is now a fully licenced Public House on the northernmost plot leased to Hull Trinity House which cannot be necessary to that purpose for which the leases were granted.

"We understand negotiations have taken place with a view to the HCB handing over the lifeboat and rescue operation but we are told that nothing has been settled yet so in the circumstances we think it will be best that notices to quit the land at Spurn are served and we send you these notices in duplicate and we should be obliged if you will sign them and return them to us at your earliest convenience, signed by the proper person under your Act for the Humber Conservancy Board. We have given long notices advisedly so that if lands are required by HCB or those to whom they have given their powers for life saving purposes, applications may be made to Constable Settled Estates, but it must be understood that upon discussion of terms of letting, power will not be given to sub let."

A letter from Commander Atkin to Mr. Franklin marked CONFIDENTIAL thanked Franklin for his letter with particulars about the lifeboat and the offical notice to quit Spurn for the lifeboat establishment. Franklin had signed the document giving the notice and had sent a copy to Atkin who could not conceal his delight. He had been in touch with W. S. Wright who shared Atkin's joy.

Franklin wrote to Andrew M. Jackson, the HCB's Solicitor, to tell him the news and who would deal with the legal complexities. Franklin hurriedly sent out notices to quit to every person living at Spurn mentioning that the Humber Conservancy Board had been given notice to quit by Constable Settled Estates and it was no fault of the HCB. I doubt if anyone really believed this unlikely lie for it was common knowledge in the local area that the HCB didn't want anything to do with the lifeboat establishment at Spurn so the story put about by the HCB had a very hollow ring to it. However, the notice to quit was genuine enough and had to be heeded.

The BOT were horrified. Mr. Pelham was doing his best about a bad job and he now felt HCB were going to get away with murder.

Letters to Franklin from the Admiralty and Lloyds voiced their dismay although Franklin had intimated that perhaps the Solicitors acting for Constable Settled Estates would look kindly at proposals to renew individual leases. He wasn't offering any help in this situation. Franklin gave the Admiralty and Lloyds details of how to contact the Constable Settled Estates and these two bodies instructed their legal advisers to negotiate new leases from the owner of the land.

The notice to quit their cottages sent to the lifeboat crew at Spurn, together with termination of their employment as lifeboat crew members, brought a considerable amount of worry and anxiety to these simple but gallant people. They had been caught up in the power game enjoyed by the HCB and would suffer the most. Letters from some of them were heart-rending and it is nice to know that most of these people were able to negotiate new leases with the Constable Estate.

One particular letter from the schoolmaster, who had served at Spurn for $15\frac{1}{2}$ years and hadn't anywhere to go, asked the HCB for a job. Franklin told him he would put his request on the agenda at the next meeting for consideration but no record tells us of the outcome although I believe the school carried on with another lease from Constable Estates.

Letters from Franklin to Mr. Hopper, who had the licence of the Lifeboat Inn, were rather protracted. Hopper proved rather more adept at bargaining than Franklin imagined but he was persuaded to approach Constable Estates in the end.

Wright and Atkin were rubbing their hands with glee at the thoughts of getting rid of the dratted lifeboat and the crew. They had had to pay these men for over 2 years and in spite of their protests would have to carry on with the largesse until the HCB lease ran out in May 1911.

Wright had emphasised at the next Board Meeting that they had offered a payment toward the upkeep of the lifeboat operation, at the Board of Trade's insistence and the RNLI had offered sometime ago to contribute £150 towards the burden of maintenance if the HCB would continue to run the service.

So now the Board of Trade had to work on the previously reluctant RNLI to persuade them to take over and operate the lifeboat establishment. The sum of £150 would help with the average expense of £460 which was accepted as the yearly outlay to retain the lifeboat service. Formal notices to quit premises at Spurn were sent to all residents on 8th June 1910.

In the meantime Franklin had sent Mr. Pelham the details of all lifeboat activities for the last 10 years.

A letter was received from John B. Trapper-Lomax, Major Chichester-Constable's Agent, to Franklin saying that he had a list of former tenants of premises on Spurn and asked for new leases and he would be grateful if Franklin could give him a list of former tenants of premises on Spurn.

A letter from the Rev. C. M. Barnes, the clergyman who looked after the Spiritual needs at Spurn, to Franklin said that he hoped the lifeboat would be retained as its departure would be a disaster.

Press cuttings, Eastern Morning News June 25th 1910 regarding dismissal of lifeboat men etc and a cutting from Eastern Morning News dated June 27th 1910 showing a letter from one 'Seafarer' whose letter was very pertinent and hard hitting. Franklin didn't like letters like that and in some cases didn't pass them on to Wright and Atkin.

Letter from Thomas Pelham BOT to Franklin asked for details of the numbers of cases of salvage of property of vessels successfully got off or assisted and of lives saved during last 10 years.

A letter from Mr. Inglefield of Lloyds of London to Franklin acknowledged receipt of termination of tenure at Spurn forwarded by Lloyds local agent, Brown Atkinson & Co. Ltd., requiring Lloyds to discontinue use of flagpole and store on Spurn Head. However, Lloyds went on to inform HCB in no uncertain terms that they regarded the proposed disestablishment of the lifeboat facility at Spurn would severely inconvenience the progress of shipping in the Humber estuary, and that they resented such a short period of notice. They went on to inform HCB that they were intent on negotiating with Constable Settled Estates to secure a new lease and they would be very grateful if they could stay at Spurn until May 1911 when the HCB lease of tenure terminated.

A letter from Commander Atkin to Franklin dated July 12th 1910 asked if there were any other means available to carry out salvage operations had the lifeboat not been available, and under the same conditions would not the lives have been equally safe?

A letter to Mr. Pelham (BOT) from Mr. Franklin (HCB) dated 13th July 1910 giving details asked for by BOT ex Spurn. During previous 10 years the number of cases of salvage of property of vessels successfully got off or assisted was 19, number of lives saved during same period was 59.

In some cases however, it is fair to assume that rescue could have been undertaken without the assistance of the lifeboat but very few of these occasions were noted.

A letter from the British Shipmaster's Association local branch in Hull, dated 13th July 1910 voiced their very grave concern at the proposed abandonment of thelifeboat station and wished to register their protests, they gave their intention of laying their grave concern before the Board of Trade and the local Chamber of Commerce and made the point that the lifeboat at Spurn, situated inside the Humber and always afloat, was available when neighbouring lifeboats were unable to put out to sea, and considering the great number of passengers who travelled to and from the Continent through the Humber Ports, the Master Mariners of Hull would view with apprehension any abolition of a lifeboat stationed in such a favourable position for carrying out the purpose of saving life.

However, in a letter from Alfred Franklin to Commander Atkin, Mr. Franklin referred to the figures described above as misleading and that he felt that more emphasis should be made to make a case for diluting the effect of the lifeboat's availability and to so denigrate the work and efforts of such brave and gallant men, he went on to say that Messrs. Stamp, Jackson and Birk were anxious to save Major Chichester-Constable the 'odium' of abolishing the lifeboat facilities.

Newspaper cuttings from the 'Eastern Morning News' spoke of the details of the HCB Board Meeting of 13th July 1910 and gave a report, also cutting from 'Daily Mail' with a letter from William Hewson protesting about rumours of the lifeboat abandonment. This gentleman obviously knew the HCB of old because he went on to slam their methods and practices.

A further newspaper cutting dated 15th July from the Eastern Morning News covering the same Board Meeting and Mr. W. S. Wright's pronouncement that the RNLI should take over the lifeboat operation at Spurn as they were the proper organisation to do the job.

Lloyds of London, in a letter to Franklin dated 15th July advised that they were now negotiating with Constable Settled Estates for a new lease but they thanked the HCB for allowing them to stay at Spurn until May 11th when the HCB's tenure expired.

In a letter dated 16th July to Commander Atkins, Franklin thanked him for the two letters of a personal nature concerning the Spurn Lifeboat Station, Franklin became rather sarcastic when he mentioned the letter from William Hewson that appeared in the local Newspaper. He declared that "Nobody takes any notice of this man's letters and no one ever replies or takes issue with his opinions", there was no doubt that the HCB's policy was correct, Franklin affirmed. He accused David Pye, the Spurn Coxswain, of not attending to requests for information promptly. He also accused Messrs. Stamp, Jackson and Birks of misleading the HCB, and observed that Major Chichester-Constable and his agent Mr. John Trapper-Lomax had visited Spurn recently and inspected the cottages and other buildings.

Mr. Franklin spoke of the contentious Board Meetings which was reported in the local newspaper and the question from Captain Taylor concerning a letter that was supposed to be on the way to Mr. Franklin from the local Shipmaster's Association, Franklin scoffed "I have not received such a letter, but I have heard that their secretary has been instructed to send me one, so far nothing has arrived".

Another letter from Commander Atkin to Franklin dated 15th July concerning Messrs. Stamp, Jackson and Birks, when he speculated if this firm of Solicitors were the proper people to bear the odium of discontinuing the lifeboat service?

A letter was received from a Joseph Webster, the School Master at Spurn, who was very concerned that the school was likely to be closed. He, Mr. Webster, would be thrown out of his job and he had served the school for $15\frac{1}{2}$ years. Could the HCB offer him a job at Spurn or Hull? He said he was well known to the Elder Brethren of Hull Trinity House.

A succession of letters to David Pye and members of the lifeboat crew at Spurn giving them notice of the termination of their contract of employment, one can imagine the reaction of these men on receiving such news.

The situation at Spurn certainly looked bleak at this moment. The continued worry about the uncertainty of the prolonged existence of the Lifeboat Station and the crew. Mr. Pye couldn't help with much information as regard the future. He had had enought problems trying to get news from the HCB and he fervently hoped that the whole unpleasant matter would be sorted out one way or the other for everyone's sake.

Mr. T. E. Blythe, a member of the lifeboat crew, wrote to Franklin to ask if he could stay in his cottage, as he hadn't been at Spurn long and he had been put to great expense with a move from Cromer. I hope the HCB had some charity!

Mr. Ormsby-Jones wrote to Franklin on August 11th 1910, advising him that a Mr. Garnham Roper of the Board of Trade in London was visiting Filey and he would like to see him while he was in the area, also could Franklin arrange a trip for him to go to Spurn so he could view the area.

Mr. Pelham of the London Board fo Trade wrote to Franklin on August 11th with reference to the Humber Conservancy Boards determination to abolish the Spurn Lifeboat Station. After careful examination of the situation the Board of Trade were of the opinion, that in the interests of safety to Shipping it was necessary to discover some means whereby the establishment might be kept up. The Board of Trade had established contact with the agent of Major Chichester-Constable to learn if negotiations could begin to arrange another lease, thus safeguarding the lifeboat station. However, time was necessary to discuss and negotiate so the result of our efforts could not be known before the beginning of Spetmember.

Alfred Franklin wrote to the local branch of the British Shipmaster's Association in Hull in reply to their letter of concern and protest as follows:-

"Regarding your letter of protest concerning the proposed abandonment of the Spurn Lifeboat, this decision has been forced on the HCB by Constable Settled Estates termination of our leases, so obviously the lifeboat and crew are affected. You will see that the HCB have had no option in this matter".

What a damned lie, what a mutilation of the facts. Why did a wealthy, influential body like the Humber Conservancy Board resort to downright lies? We know that far beyond Constable Settled Estates giving the HCB notice to quit that both Wright and Atkin were determined to get rid of the lifeboat establishment at Spurn, why distort the truth in such a blatant way?

Mr. Garnham Roper had visited Spurn and enjoyed his trip and look round. I wonder if the BOT were aware of the lies and deceit practised by the HCB?

As a token of magnaminity, the HCB agreed to extend the leases on Spurn until their tenure expired.

Newspaper cutting dated Friday September 9th 1910 of the 'Eastern Morning News' mentions Mr. Garnham Roper's visit to Spurn and the HCB's intention of allowing lifeboat and crew to remain at Spurn until satisfactory arrangements had been concluded between the Board of Trade and Constable Settled Estates.

Mr. Ormsby-Jones asked for update of situation regarding Spurn Lifeboat on 12th September.

Mr. W. S. Wright, in a letter to Mr. Franklin in a reply, stated, "I think it desirable that the request of the Board of Trade with regard to the Spurn lifeboat should be agreed to, and I agree with Commander Atkin that the BOT should be informed that HCB agrees to allow the lifeboat and crew to remain in situ until the last day of our tenure at Spurn (May 11th), to facilitate their negotiations with Constable Settled Estates and that it must not be taken as a departure in any way from the position which the HCB has taken up with regard to this matter or as involving any responsibility for the lifeboat establishment's continued maintenance".

Mr. Franklin wrote to Mr. Pelham outlining Mr. W. S. Wright's instructions and statement, on 16th August.

On December 1st 1910 Mr. Thomas Pelham of the Board of Trade in London wrote to Franklin "With reference to the HCB letter of 12th November last, I am directed by the BOT to state that learning that HCB has decided that in no circumstances to continue to support the lifeboat establishment at Spurn, the BOT entered into negotiations with Major R. Chichester-Constable.

Discussion followed as to the conditions that he would be willing to grant new leases on the land at Spurn.

As a result of informal communications that have passed, Major Chichester-Constable made a provisional offer which appeared to the Board of Trade as being very reasonable.

Before proceeding any further the BOT were glad to

learn in the event of this offer being accepted, the HCB would be willing to contribute towards the maintenance of the Lifeboat Station the sum of £200 per annum which the BOT understands from unofficial communication which have passed between the BOT and the HCB, the latter would be willing to contribute, the balance being provided by the RNLI and HM Government.

In a letter from Franklin to Atkin discussing Mr. Pelham's points of importance, Franklin makes the following comments:-

"You will see from Pelham's letter that the sum which he suggests the HCB should pay towards the maintenance of the Lifeboat Station is £200 per annum. I must say at once that I do not remember this figure of £200 being mentioned by anyone at the HCB. £150 yes, was suggested by the RNLI. I am sending copies of Pelham's letter to our chairman."

But in letter to Franklin from W. S. Wright on 3rd December, Mr. Wright was pleased to see that the lifeboat problem was now almost settled. He had talked with Commander Atkin and he thought it might be possible to pay the £200 suggested by Mr. Pelham.

Commander Atkin replied on December 5th, to Franklin, thanking him for the copy of Mr. Pelham's letter on the question of the Spurn Lifeboat. Commander Atkin noted the reference to the £200 which was required as a contribution to help to maintain the lifeboat operation at Spurn, but he pointed out that htis sum was the very extreme as far as the HCB was concerned. He thought "That we shall be well out of the matter by payment of such a sum".

The year 1911 marked the final stage of the Humber Conservancy Board's control of the destinies of the Spurn Lifeboat Station. In spite of the far from satisfactory notions of Messrs. Atkin and Wright, one must give them some credit for the way that they did pay the crew and maintain the establishment albeit very reluctantly.

The fact that the HCB were still hellbent on washing their hands of the whole lifeboat operation and to the very end of their tenure they never lost an opportunity to discredit the necessity of the presence of the establishment.

On the other hand, a certain amount of self congratulations were celebrated at the good fortune that Major Chichester-Constable's notice to quit had brought them. This stroke of luck had not gone unnoticed in Hull and there were many who saw through this charade. The Board of Trade must be given great credit for their efforts to achieve a satisfactory settlement of this thorny problem, there must have been many occasions when Thomas Pelham, the Secretary of the Board of Trade, wrung his hands in desperation when Messrs. Atkin and Wright refused point blank to listen to reason and showed a great degree of stubbornness.

However, Mr. Pelham would be the first to admit that circumstances had worked out well in the end with the impending take over of the lifeboat operation by the obvious body, the RNLI. Public opinion was voluble in its opinion that the RNLI would run the lifeboat station efficiently and without outside interference.

The lifeboat Coxswain and crew were delighted at the prospect of the RNLI takeover. They had all expressed a willingness to carry on in the employ of the new masters, and thought that more financial appreciation might be shown to them. They hadn't had a pay rise for many years and in spite of overtures being directed toward the Humber Conservancy Board, no response was forthcoming.

The flow of correspondence between the HCB and the RNLI and the mediator, the Board of Trade in London, continued unabated. Most of the stilted letters were made up of acknowledgements and reminders, even in those days letters were duplicated and often unnecessary. On January 4th 1911, a letter from Mr. J. Hopper, who ran the Lifeboat Inn at Spurn, asked Mr. Franklin if he could stay on at the Inn until the end of the HCB's tenure of lease.

A letter from Mr. Franklin to David Pye, the Coxswain at Spurn, on January 14th enclosed a newspaper cutting from the Hull Daily Mail of January 12th 1911, alleging that the schooner 'Hilda' ran aground on the Stony Binks on the night of January 11th and that her distress signals were not observed by the lifeboat lookouts and crew.

Mr. Franklin remarked that the Marine Committee of the Humber Conservancy Board would desire to have information about this incident and therefore Mr. Pye's observations would be required as soon as possible!

Another newspaper cutting from the Eastern Morning News of January 13th described the stranding and subsequent salvage of the 'Hilda'. A letter from Andrew M. Jackson, the Solicitor to the HCB, commented on the disgraceful neglect of duty by the Coxswain and Crew of the Spurn Lifeboat when the 'Hilda's distress signals were ignored. Mr. Jackson went on to intimate that the sooner the HCB were no longer responsible for the lifeboat, the better.

However, a letter from David Pye, the Coxswain of the Spurn Lifeboat, gave a very different picture of the incident. This letter was sent on 17th January and was supported by evidence from onlookers at Grimsby Fish Docks who saw the 'Hilda' run aground on Clee Ness sands. Mr. PYe then gave his detailed report on the stranding:-

"Dear Sir,

Your letter to hand, I do not think the report in the paper is one from the Captain of the 'Hilda'. I do not think that anyone would try to put a vessel on the Binks in such weather as we had at the time mentioned.

A vessel would not have lasted very long, it would have been a very poor chance for the crew in such a sea. A proper watch was kept throughout the night and none of the men saw a flare. I was in the Watch House myself until very late the same night and no flare was shown. Just about day break on January 12th, I noticed the vessel mentioned sailing up the Humber at the S.W. side of the Bull Sand and she appeared to be alright. After sailing some distance, the vessel was put about and sailed back towards the Bull Lightship.

Whilst coming down on the S.W. side of the Bull Sand, a flag was hoisted to the mast head and when near the Lightship it was lowered to half mast and went just to the South East of the Lightship. Then the vessel was put about and sailed back again up the River and stranded on the Clee Ness Sand. I knew it was no use me commencing to sail after her as she was going faster than we could have sailed and she was going into smooth water all the time. In the Humber at that time were tugs and trawlers lying about.

I saw the vessel sail onto the Clee Ness Sand and the tug 'Kimberly' go to the vessel and I saw the crew of the 'Hilda' leave in their own boat and the tug picked them up near to the ship.

I do not believe that the vessel had been on the Binks. If any flares had been shown we should have proceeded to the vessel and have rendered what assistance we could, as we alway have in the past."

The report in the Eastern Morning News of January 13th was as follows:-

Exciting scenes were witnessed from the Grimsby Pontoon yesterday, when the Brigantine 'Hilda', which had sprung a leak in the North Sea, drove into the Humber and was beached. The crew were taken off by the Grimsby tug 'Kimberly'.

When the Brigantine drove into the Humber, it was seen that she was flying signals of distress and was labouring very heavily. Her head was pointed for the Clee Ness bank, and she drove ashore in a blinding blizzard. Her signal was altered to "Want a Tug" and immediately the tugs 'Kimberly' and 'Solway' put off to her assistance, while the Lifeboat crew summoned and were ready to launch their boat. (this would have been the Grimsby Lifeboat based in the Royal Dock Basin).

Heavy seas broke over the vessel as she drove nearer in shore but the 'Kimberly', getting close up to her, was able to take the crew on board and bring them into Grimsby.

The Captain, in an interview, said his vessel was the 'Hilda' of Faversham, bound from that port to Stockton with a cargo of old iron. She sprang a leak in the North Sea on Wednesday night and as she was filling rapidly, his only chance was to make for the Humber.

But the water gained rapidly on the pumps and when the 'Hilda' was almost sinking, he had to beach her.

The crew were able to save some of their belongs, but everything else on board will, it is feared, be lost.

The rising tide coming in with a gale behind it threatened to break the vessel up at any moment and it was thought, judging from her position that she will be a total wreck."

Mr. Andrew M. Jackson, who as the Solicitor to the Humber Conservancy Board, shared both Atkin and Wrights feelings that the lifeboat establishment should be abolished as soon as possible, was very quick to notice the report in the Hull Daily Mail telling of the far from authentic tale that the 'Hilda' had run aground on the Stony Binks and that her distress flares had been ignored by the men on Watch at Spurn Lifeboat Station. He advised Atkin to drag Pye before the Committee of the HCB and demand an explanation.

What a pity that these so called public minded pillars of society and industry did not arrange their facts in the correct order. Pye's report was detailed and accurate and puts to shame the accusations and lies that had been manufactured to try to heap discredit onto the Spurn Lifeboat Station. As it happened, the onlookers on the Grimsby Pontoon had seen the incident before their very eyes and their evidence could not have been denied.

No doubt the HCB would have to digest the facts and not the unfounded rumours, which were unworthy of such prominent Hull business men.

If the ficticious reports about the 'Hilda' grounding on the Binks were another clumsy attempt to discredit the Coxswain and crew of the lifeboat, whoever was foolish enough to spread such rumours, especially to the local press, did the lifeboat crew more favours than damage. Anyone who knew of the dedication and courage of the Spurn Lifeboat crew realised that dark forces were trying to dismiss any credit that would enhance the reputation of the lifeboat's credibility. However, soon the lifeboat establishment would be placed in more reliable, caring hands who would be free from any petty ideas of destroying reputations.

Various letters from BOT and HCB concerning the arrangement for paying the £200 by HCB to RNLI. Apparently everything had to be spelled out in words of one syllable to convince the RNLI and the BOT. Atkin couldn't wait for the transfer of responsibilities from HCB to RNLI and he wrote to Franklin on February 4th whining that he wished that BOT would hurry up and approve the RNLI takeover as the HCB tenancy of the Cottages at Spurn expired shortly and what would he do then?

A letter from Clayton, Sons and Fargus, Solicitors, who represented the RNLI, to Mr. Franklin at the HCB, confirmed that RNLI would be taking over all the responsibilities for the Lifeboat Station at Spurn. It was noted that the School, Post Office and Lifeboat house had been hitherto rented from Constable Settled Estates for the magnificent sum of £5 per annum. No doubt this annual rent would be reviewed under the new draft lease being negotiated by the RNLI and Major Chichester-Constable.

Clayton, Sons, and Fargus noted with satisfaction that the present lifeboat crew were agreeable to continue their employment under the RNLI.

A Telegraphic message from Captain Holmes, RNLI on 20th March 1911 to Mr. Franklin at the HCB asking if he could make an appointment with Franklin to discuss the impending takeover of the lifeboat establishment.

Mr. Franklin wrote back to Clayton, Sons, and Fargus in reply to their letter stating that as far as HCB were concerned the HCB connection with the lifeboat operation would cease on May 1st 1911 when their lease expired. The lifeboatmen would be given notice that their employment would be terminated on the same date but HCB understood that RNLI were taking them on thus achieving continuity under possible new conditions of service.

Mr. Franklin wrote to the Director of Works at the Admiralty in London on 24th March advising them that HCB's lease expired on May 1st next and HCB assumed that the Admiralty had entered into negotiations with Major Chichester-Constable for a new agreement for the tenancy of the signal station when the HCB lease ran out.

A similar letter was sent to Lloyds of London and the Rev. C. M. Barnes, Easington, to advise of the importance of preparing for future tenancies at Spurn.

Mr. D. Pye, Coxwain at Spurn, received a letter from Mr. Franklin on March 24th telling him that Captain Holmes RNLI and his assistant Inspector Hall intended to visit Spurn and talk to the residents and lifeboat crew about the imminent takeover by the RNLI. A few days later Mr. Pye wrote back to Franklin informing him that the visit had taken place and everything had been amicable.

Captain Holmes also wrote to Mr. Franklin to report on his trip to Spurn. He, too, seemed pleased with the attitude of all concerned. It would seem that the lifeboat crew had appeared relieved that their jobs were safe and that the new conditions of service were acceptable. Captain Holmes referred to the school, which was a Church School under the East Riding Education Authority and the correspondent was the Rev. C. M. Barnes of Easington Parish. Captain Holmes would be grateful to examine any agreement between the HCB and the School Managers. The Post Office was located in a room of Mr. Pye's home and the Post Mistress, Miss Hopper, was of course a Post Office official and was paid as such. Again, if any agreements between the HCB and the GPO were available, the RNLI would like to peruse them.

Mr. Franklin replied on March 27th and enclosed the relevant documents that Captain Holmes requested. As regard the school, a rent of 1/- per year was paid. No agreement was in force concerning the Post Office, but there may have been some arrangement in existence between Mr. Pye and the Post Office.

An anguished letter from Lloyds of London on 27th March wailing that they had been in touch with Mr. Trapper-Lomax, (Mr. Chichester-Constable's Agent), regarding a new lease for the signal station at Spurn but had not received a reply as yet.

A series of formal notices to Members of the lifeboat crew to inform them of the termination of appointments with HCB and requesting return of signed acceptances.

The transfer of obligations to the RNLI seemed fraught with anomalies. As in most complex change of responsibilities, the HCB behaved like an Old Woman in Red Bloomers. Such concern for the most trivial point, bringing back the threat of 'Disestablishment of the Lifeboat operation at once', over reaction indeed. My sympathies were with the Board of Trade who tried so hard to get the HCB and the RNLI together and their offers of mediation paid off amid the suspicion and distrust.

On the extremities, we had the nub of the problem, the lifeboat, its Coxswain and crew who wondered just what was happening to them and their livelihood. They were told very little by anyone, Mr. Pye, the Coxswain, was informed by Mr. Franklin of fragments of information, but only the crumbs of any discussion, so while the lifeboat was always available for assistance to any vessel in distress in the vicinity of Spurn, their fate was far from secure while the HCB had control.

The remainder of the correspondence between the HCB and the RNLI was taken up by queries and reminders of draft contract and arbitary clauses inserted by Mr. Andrew M. Jackson, so as to sew the transfer up tight for the future peace of mind of Messrs. Atkin and Wright.

A Newspaper report in the Eastern Morning News of 26th April 1911 stated the following:-

"The Secretary of Hull Chamber of Commerce, Mr. J. Gregson, has issued a circular stating that arrangement have been made for a night watch to be kept at Spurn Signal Station when required from the above date for the purpose of reporting inward and outward bound vessels outside the official hours on the following conditions.

The Watch shall only be kept on intimation being given to the signalman at Spurn (Mr. Hopper) of the expectation of a vessel passing and requiring to be signalled.

The fee for the night watch to be 5/- per vessel, plus cost of message.

Should a watch be kept and the vessel subsequently passes during official day hours, the night watch fee is to be paid.

Particulars of the Night Signals of the said vessels or vessel to be sent to the Signalman at Spurn."

A letter from Mr. Franklin to Captain Holmes regarding the examination and possible overhaul of the moorings at Spurn which the RNLI felt needed examination. Mr. Franklin, after making enquiries of the chief engineer of the HCB, felt obliged to inform Captain Holmes that the HCB was not equipped for such work but did recommend two firms in Hull that might be interested.

So on May 1st 1911 there ended 3 years of argument, bitterness and mistrust between the Humber Conservancy Board, who should have known better, the RNLI, who should have accepted responsibility from the beginning; the Board of Trade in London under whose good council and patience a settlement was achieved for everyone's good. Luckily, the lifeboat service survived such unpleasantness and offered its availability to ships using the Humber. However, the ever present threat from Messrs. Atkin and Wright to abandon the facility remained like a Sword of Damocles over them.

The Humber Estuary was witnessing the development of the growing fishing industry in Hull and Grimsby. Commercial Shipping was finding the Humber ports keen to offload and take on board all manners of cargo. The River Humber was well known and its potential was being realised in those years between 1908 and 1911. In view of the very much increased trade using the grey wastes of the river, one could not entertain any thought of disestablishing an essential service such as the lifeboat at Spurn Point. It seems inconcievable that the lifeboat service was nearly dispensed with owing to the obsession of the Humber Conservancy Board. If one considers the risks taken in the inclement weather conditions, amid the shoals and myriad currents that scatter across the mouth of the River, the Stony Binks, ever present to trap the unlucky vessel on its gravel bank, Trinity Sands, too, welcomed the unwary mariner who lost his bearings in a winter's storm. Such were the problems which beset the seafarer entering the Humber and such were the calls for assistance rendered by the gallant men who manned the lifeboat at Spurn in those far off days and to whom the unlucky victim of a vessel in distress turned to with their flares and red flag at the mast head.

All the above mentioned facts give a very clear indication of the necessity of maintaining the lifeboat at Spurn Point, let no one believe that such a service fulfilled a less essential function without which countless seagoing folk would have shared a watery grave. At least the lifeboat operation gave them a chance to remove the availability of the lifeboat's assistance, would be nothing short of criminal.

One cannot explain what got into the minds of the men who operated the Humber Conservancy Board, who were appointed to their positions of trust by Central Government, and whom the public respected. Was it just that they were against paying the full time crew? Why did the RNLI, in all their glory, who proudly claimed to look after the people in a stricken vessel by their lifeboat's readiness to go to assist ANY vessel in difficulties, object to the responsibility of paying the full time crew at Spurn? The RNLI could afford to pay and would have been accorded recognition and grateful thanks.

Answers to such questions will now never be known, all we do know is that the Spurn Lifeboat survived such troubles and gained strength by the actions of a dedicated Cox and crew. Such men were above the petty quarrels and politics of people who should have known better.

Certainly the RNLI's influence was readily accepted and conditions at Spurn became more settled and secure. No more back biting, no more bickering, in fact, life settle down to a well ordered existence under the RNLI.

However, with the HCB's £200 and the BOT's £150, the RNLI had solid financial support for the continuance of a Lifeboat Station.

CHAPTER FOUR

THE DAWN OF THE RNLI ERA

The month of May 1911 was an important time for the Coxswain and crew of the Spurn Point Lifeboat Station.

At last the stranglehold exerted by the Humber Conservancy Board had been broken and the lifeboat operation had passed into the welcoming arms of the Royal National Lifeboat Institution, who had the experience, know how and attitude to estabish harmony and efficiency among the men who manned the Spurn Point Lifeboat Station.

Records do not show details of life at Spurn in those early days under the RNLI's control but one could imagine a far more relaxed and happier atmosphere existed under the new regime.

However, life went on and the operation of the lifeboat continued as usual. The RNLI's methods of improvement and updating were gradual, the crew were, of course, still full time employed, and received the wages commensurate with such a status. These payments would be increased at intervals at the RNLI's discretion. The Coxswain's designation was Superintendent Coxswain, there being no Honorary Secretary, as the full time basis of employment was unique and thus the Coxswain had full powers to administer the full running of the station.

David Pye, the Coxswaim, who had shouldered the burden of Coxswain during the unpleasant rule of the Humber Conservancy Board and had been a tower of strength at Spurn for many years, retired in 1912. This gentleman had perhaps the worst possible problems during the Humber Conservancy Boards reign, he had to try to instil confidence and reassurance into the doubting minds of the crew during those uncertain times when the crew didn't know whether they were coming or going, such was the interference thrust upon them by the wiles and machinations of the men in charge of the Humber Conservancy Board. Mr. Pye's tenure of office was to some extent submerged in this welter of intolerance, but his qualities of leadership were never in doubt and he was respected by the crew as a kind, intelligent man who really wanted to be left alone to run the operation. And I expect the possibility of being able to hand over the job as Superintendent Coxswain to a popular member of the crew like Robert Cross came as a welcome relief.

Robert Cross had been a member of the crew of the Spurn Point Lifeboat for 6 years prior to being appointed as Superintendent Coxswain in 1912. His appointment was welcomed by the crew who felt that he was one of them and they had seen the qualities of leadership develop over the years. Robert Cross would make his mark as one of the bravest Coxswains in the RNLI for when he retired in 1943 at the age of 67 he had been in charge for 31 years and had taken part in the rescue of 403 lives, had won the RNLI Gold Medal twice, the RNLI Silver Medal 3 times, the Bronze Medal twice, and Thanks on Vellum and the George Medal. During his 6 years as a member of the crew before the RNLI took over the station he had taken part in the rescue of 50 lives and so his grand total of saving lives is 453.

Records do not show much rescue activity at Spurn during the period May 1911 until 13th January 1913. It should be emphasised that the longer a lifeboat is inactive, apart from training routines, nobody's life is at risk. It is often remarked upon that "The Lifeboat hasn't been called out very often in this or that period" without understanding the good reason that the RNLI is available when needed.

As an illustration, when the first Cleethorpes Lifeboat 'The Manchester Unity' arrived at the station, she was not called out for rescue purposes until 2 years later. Alternatively, a lifeboat may be called out every day of the week or once a year.

The RNLI Journal, 'The Lifeboat', reveals that on January 13th 1913 the Spurn Lifeboat, now using the more modern lifeboat named 'Charles Deere James' which had replaced the former ex-Hull Trinity House boat, had been called out as follows:-

"During very dense fog conditions, signals of distress were heard from a Steamer, most probably the sounds of a steam siren, and it was thought that she was ashore on the Inner Binks. The lifeboat was launched and she proceeded along the edge of the sands for about 2 miles.

At the time of the launch the Steamer's siren sounded continuously, but they ceased, and the lifeboat was not able to find the vessel.

The lifeboat, therefore returned ashore, this was about 5pm. Shortly afterwards the fog lifted a little and the grounded vessel continued to sound her siren. The 'Charles Deere James' again proceeded to sea and on reaching the vessel which had succeeded in getting clear of the sands, the lifeboat Cox was informed by the Master of the vessel that they had lost their propellor and that she required a tug. The lifeboat stood by the ship, which as identified as the steam trawler 'CANCER' of Grimsby, until the tug arrived and the danger was passed. The lifeboat then returned to shore.

Six days later, the new Spurn Lifeboat was called out when the watchman reported that a vessel had stranded on the 'Inner Binks' about 1 mile S.E. of the watch house. Robert Cross, the Superintendent Coxswain of the lifeboat, went to the watch house and perceiving that the vessel was in a dangerous position and likely to drift further onto the bank, immediately summoned the crew and launched the lifeboat.

When nearing the stricken vessel, it was found that she had, in fact, driven over the sandbank and was on the inner side.

The lifeboat got as near as possible and connection was effected by means of the heaving cane and line. The lifeboat was made fast and she eventually succeeded in saving the vessel which proved to be barge 'CAMBRIA' of London, bound for Gainsborough with a cargo of manure. There was a strong S.S.E. breeze blowing at the time and the sea conditions were rough.

The next recorded call for help was 11 months later on December 8th 1913, and by this time the Cox and crew

had moulded themselves into a highly proficient and reliable unit. The 'Charles Deere James' was a big improvement on the old Trinity House craft and they felt they could now cope with any type of rescue with confidence, so it was with some satisfaction that at 7.30am on December 8th in a period of dense fog that the watchman reported that a vessel was ashore on the beach, about one mile to the mast of the watch house.

The crew of the lifeboat were summoned at once and proceeded in the small boarding boat to 'the assistance of the vessel which was identified as the motor fishing vessel 'PAT' of Grimsby bound for the fishing grounds. With the assistance of the lifeboat crew the 'PAT' was refloated and she returned to Grimsby.

It is relevant that at the time of this call for assistance, the wind was light but there was a nasty ground swell and had it not been for the timely assistance rendered to the vessel she would have become a total wreck.

The 'Charles Deere James' was called to the assistance of the Steamer 'Balvenie' of Glasgow in the early hours of February 7th 1914. The 'Balvenie', whilst bound for Grangemouth from Grimsby with a cargo of pig iron, rang aground on the 'Inner Binks'. When she first struck the banks, the weather was moderately fine but about 5.45am the wind freshened and the ship found herself in a position of considerable danger.

The Spurn Lifeboat was launched to go to assist the steamer and stood by until about 1pm when the 'Balvenie' succeeded in refloating. By this time a moderate gale was blowing and the Ship's Captain expressed his appreciation of the services performed by the lifeboat and crew in standing by the steamer until she was out of danger.

On March 25th 1914 the services of the Spurn Lifeboat were required when it was reported that the BULL light vessel was firing rockets and in response the crew of the 'Charles Deere James' were assembled and the lifeboat was launched and went to the light vessel. On arrival it was found that a collision had occurred between the Norwegian Steamer 'NORRIS' outward bound, and the English Brigantine 'Jean Anderson' of Hull, bound for London from Hull with a cargo of lubricating oil.

The collision had occurred quite close to the BULL

light vessel and one of the ships had fouled the light vessel, but no damage was sustained and the light vessel did not require any assistance.

The lifeboat then proceeded to the brigantine and her Captain asked Coxswain Cross to stand by and if possible save the vessel, as she was making water fast. Her bows had been completely cut off to the water line. Four of the crew of the 'Charles Deere James' were transferred to the brigantine to help man the pumps and the lifeboat remained in close attendance while the stricken vessel was laboriously towed to Grimsby by the 'Norris'. At Grimsby a tug towed the brigantine across to Hull. The 4 lifeboatmen remained on board, but the 'Charles Deere James' returned to her station.

In the first months of the Great War, the services of the Spurn Lifeboat were needed more than ever. Apart from the ever present dangers of the weather, wind, and sea, there was a new menace, the mine, which added to the travails and hazards of ships at sea.

Besides the uncertainty of the weather, there was the ever present, although unpredictable, problems of enemy action which would require more rescue attempts by the RNLI to help the unfortunates who survived the results of warfare at sea.

The first occurence of rescue in the the Great War came on September 9th 1914, when the Sloop 'Chesterfield', whilst bound for Hull from Kings Lynn laden with gravel, got herself stranded on the notorious Inner Binks. Coxswain Cross immediately assembled his crew and proceeded to the vessel in the small boarding lifeboat. On arrival it was found that the sea was sweeping right over the Sloop and she was filling with water. The Sloop's small boat which had been launched was almost immediately swamped. As the 3 men on board were in considerable danger owing to the heavy ground swell, Coxswain Cross advised them to abandon their ship without delay. They took his advice and very shortly they were taken aboard the small lifeboat, and watched with sadness as the 'Chesterfield' was broken up by the pounding seas.

On October 29th of 1914 the Middle Binks threatened the very existence of the Schooner 'Union' of Portsmouth when she ran aground on the gravel banks. The 'Charles Deere James' was launched and proceeded to the rescue. The Schooner was found to be labouring heavily with the sea breaking over her. The lifeboat anchored and veered down until she was near enough to get a line aboard and stood by until the Schooner managed to refloat herself.

The Spurn Lifeboat then accompanied the 'Union' until she reached a safe anchorage. Not quite the end of the story though, a strong E.N.E. gale was blowing with a very heavy sea at the time of the rescue and owing to the force of the wind the lifeboat was not able to get back to her moorings until the next day.

So far we have witnessed the willingness of the RNLI's rescue service for ship and man operated during the Wartime Emergency. As previously mentioned, the added potential dangers did not deter the lifeboat crew and we must respect the bravery and courage of such men.

The Middle Binks again found the keel of the Steamer 'Elantsabe' of Bilbao on 2nd December 1914 when the Spurn Lifeboat was alerted to go to the aid of the Spanish vessel carrying a crew of 24 hands that had grounded on the Middle Bink whilst bound for Middlesbrough with a cargo of iron.

It was blowing a strong south westerly by west gale and a very rough sea was running. At the request of the Master of the Steamer, the Lifeboat stood by until she succeeded in freeing herself from the embraces of the gravel bank. Her Master expressed his thanks to Coxswain Cross and his crew for their services rendered.

On the morning of 15th February 1915, during a moderate northerly breeze with a heavy ground swell, a steamer was reported ashore about 1 mile north west of Donna Nook, and she was flying signals of distress. The lifeboat was launched and proceeded to the steamer which proved to be the 'CT8' and she was hard aground.

At the request of her Captain, the lifeboat passed a wire hawser to a tug which was standing by, and efforts were made to try to haul the ship into deeper water. These proved unsuccessful and as the services of the lifeboat were no longer needed she returned to her station.

However, 13 days later the 'Charles Deere James' was

called out to the aid of a vessel aground on the Inner Binks at 12.30am. The vigilant watchman had reported that a ship was ashore and so Mr. Cross assembled the crew and launched the lifeboat in a strong S.S.W. gale and heavy seas. The lifeboat attempted to reach the stranded vessel, but the heavy seas made this nearly impossible. First of all the sail was used to no avail then the oars, no good either, then a passing Torpedo Boat Destroyer was hailed and took the lifeboat in tow, hauling her well to windward. The lifeboat thus bore down on the wreck and with great difficulty got alongside. The sea had been making a clean breach over the stricken vessel and the lifeboat just arrived in time to rescue the crew of 4 hands before she sank. The vessel was the schooner 'William and Alice' of Hull carrying a cargo of iron.

Owing to her swinging spars, the lifeboatmen were exposed to great danger while performing the rescue. Another vessel had also stranded in the area on the Binks but she succeeded in getting clear without requiring assistance.

Details of the award of the Silver Medal of the RNLI to the Spurn Superintendent Coxswain Robert Cross for his part and intrepid conduct of 9th December 1917, in this case the SS 'Florence' of Stockton whilst bound from London to Newcastle with a cargo of oil stranded on the Middle Binks near Spurn. It was a very dark night and blowing a strong gale with a terrible sea running across the sands.

The lifeboat, when nearing the stranded vessel, took the ground and was unable to get alongside. The seas were sweeping over the steamer and her crew were shouting for help.

The Coxswain, Robert Cross, seeing that it was impossible to do anything with the lifeboat so far away from the wreck, called for volunteers to jump overboard and make way through the water near enough to get a line to the imperilled men.

No man offered, so the Coxswain himself jumped into the water with a rope but he could not get to the wreck.

The crew of the lifeboat then pulled the Cox back and again he asked for a volunteer to accompany him on to the

sandbank and pay out a line to him while he made another attempt.

This time, one of the Crew named G. Martin, inspired by the Cox's bravery and example, joined him and with the assistance they managed to effect communication. Then two men stood in the sands, although at times nearly covered in water, until the whole of the stricken vessel's crew had come down the line and had been placed safely aboard the lifeboat.

This splendid behaviour and courage of Coxswain Cross and latterly, G. Martin and the whole of the lifeboat crew met with commendation on every side and the Captain of the 'Florence'.

For this momentous service, Coxswain R. Cross was awarded the Silver Medal of the RNLI and Crew member G. Martin received a Monetary Award for his part in the rescue.

Fog was a constant hazard in the winter of 1915. Potential danger from wartime contingencies added to the perils at sea but the work of the RNLI went on as usual.

The fog was at its thickest on 3rd December 1915 when signals of distress were heard and the lifeboat was launched and towed by a motor boat to the area of the Inner Binks, where they found the steamer 'Freidig' in danger of stranding after having already been on the gravel banks and refloated. The lifeboat Cox advised the Master as to the best way to get his vessel out of the dangerous position and with that assistance the 'Freidig' was able to move into deep water and resume her voyage.

At 5am on 6th December 1915, the Coastguard at Spurn reported that a steamer was sending up flares for assistance to the north of the lighthouse.

The crew of the lifeboat were assembled immediately and the boat was launched. The steamer proved to be 'Lady Ann' of Sunderland, bound from Colchester to that port in ballast. When the 'Charles Deere James' arrived under sail it was found that the crew of the steamer had provisioned the ship's lifeboats ready to abandon her.

After a discussion between the Cox of the lifeboat and the 'Lady Ann's' Master, the lifeboat remained in close attendance on the steamer until 6pm, but as she did not get off the bank on that tide, the lifeboat returned to her station and returned to the grounded vessel on the flood tide. The lifeboat then ran wire hawsers to tugs which had arrived on the scene and by this means the 'Lady Ann' was successfully refloated.

It became clear to the crew of the Spurn lifeboat that their lifeboat was just about obsolete. The 'Charles Deere James' had performed well and had given many years of good service, yet, a new type of motor powered lifeboat was gradually being introduced and inevitably Spurn would be receiving one of the "new fangled boats". To recap briefly, all manners of heroic rescue had been performed with the early rowing type lifeboats, in fact many of the rescues would be looked upon today as impossible and the quite unbelievable acts of bravery among the crew will go down in the annals of the RNLI as incredible. However, with the RNLI's tenure of control, things improved with the arrival of the more modern Watson Class 'Samuel Oakes' with the modern improvements.

In 1919, a new era of lifeboat was to unfold which would bring many new features and facilities to help the lifeboatman in his thankless task.

CHAPTER FIVE

POWER TAKES OVER

In 1919 the Spurn Point lifeboat 'Charles Deere James' was withdrawn from service at Spurn. The lifeboat had been a great improvement on the old Trinity House boat and had given reliable service to Coxswain Cross and his crew, being launched 34 times.

The Spurn Station took delivery of the 'Samuel Oakes' which had been donated to the RNLI by a legacy of Mrs. E. M. Laing of Barnes, London.

This vessel was a 'Watson' type vessel and was 40ft long by 11ft beam. She was fitted with a TYLOR petrol engine which turned out 40 SHP at a speed of 7 knots. She carried 8 oars for emergency purposes and incorporated the latest in marine design. Gone were the days of hauling on oars and wildly swinging booms. Now an internal combusion engine would enable the Cox and crew much more freedom and versatility.

The first recorded rescue involving the 'Samuel Oakes' was detailed in the 'Lifeboat Magazine' of November 1922 and referred to the 18th October 1922 when at 10pm, 2 vessels were observed to be aground and showing distress signals on the sand and gravel banks in the mouth of the Humber. The Spurn lifeboat 'Samuel Oakes' was launched and in a strong wind and frequent squalls, a heavy swell and extreme cold, she proceeded to the stranded vessels.

The first of the ships in distress was a fishing smack. She was almost submerged and only her mast was above the water. The crew were in the rigging and as the lifeboat approached, their shouts for help could be heard. A terrific sea was breaking over the sands, the worst, in the opinion of the lifeboat crew, that they had ever seen. Every now and then the sunken smack was lifted above the water and then crashed down onto the sands again. The crew of the stricken vessel were hailed and told to get ready to jump. The 'Samuel Oakes' was manoeuvred as near as possible, then the lifeboat was caught by a heavy sea and she struck the wreck. The next gigantic wave carried her clean over the wreck, but the stricken crew made no attempt to jump and it is surmised that they had lashed themselves to the rigging. The lifeboat was now right over the sandbank in a heavy broken sea and in great danger, she was constantly full of water and her crew had to cling to the mast and thwarts to prevent themselves from being washed overboard.

Before the Coxswain had got the lifeboat turned round with the intention of approaching the wreck from leeward, the mast of the wreck and all the men on the rigging had disappeared under the turbulent waves. The lifeboat cruised about for a considerable time but no sign of the men nor any of the wreckage could be found.

The 'Samuel Oakes' then made for the second wreck which was found to be the steam trawler 'Mafeking' of Hull. She also had sunk and the heavy seas were breaking over her funnel, but the crew had taken to their boats as soons as she struck the Binks and had been picked up by a pilot cutter.

The lifeboat returned to her station just after 2am and at daybreak again put out and searched the area and scene of the first wreck. However, no trace of the crew or timbers of the smack could be seen.

Had the smack's mast stood only 15 minutes longer, the Coxswain believed that the unfortunate men could have been saved. How many men were lost is not known but the smack was believed to have been Danish.

In the opinion of the RNLI Committee, this was a most dangerous and difficult service and everything that was possible was done to rescue the lives of the crew.

The RNLI Committee therefore awarded the Bronze Medal and Thanks of the Institution to Coxswain Robert Cross and their Thanks on Vellum to each of the 9 members of the lifeboat crew. In addition, the Coxswain and crew have been voted an additional monetary award.

As a diversion to their more mundane, but essential tasks, the Coxswain and crew of the Spurn lifeboat were

The steam trawler 'Mafeking' - Malcolm Fussey Photography.

invited to form a Guard of Honour for the Prince of Wales who was to visit Bradford on May 30th 1923.

A report of the visit, and the part that the Spurn lifeboat crew played in such a momentous occasion, was sent to the Editor of the 'Lifeboat Magazine by an anonymous lifeboat volunteer, and let this gentleman relate the events of the visit:-

"When the Prince of Wales visited Bradford on May 30th, the Spurn lifeboat crew, whose new motor boat is being provided out of a special fund raised in Bradford, and is to be named after the City, played a prominent part in the welcome given to him, and were themselves warmly welcomed by the people of Bradford.

They acted as part of the Guard of Honour to the Prince, as did the lifeboatmen at Swansea on his visit to that town 3 years ago.

The Spurn lifeboat crew undertook a new and pleas-

ing duty on this day in May when they acted as a Guard of Honour in the City Square at Bradford on the occasion of the visit of HRH The Prince of Wales.

The lifeboat crew travelled to Bradford on the previous day and on arrival were met by the Lord Mayor and Lady Mayoress and branch officials with whom they were photographed. Dinner was served at the Alexandra Hotel and a hearty welcome was extended to 'Bradford's Own' by Sir William Priestley, Branch Chairman; Mr. Sutcliffe Smith, Secretary; Mr. W. B. Saville; Miss Nora Grainger and others.

The crew subsequently marched to Victoria Square when Coxswain Cross laid a wreath on the local Cenetaph composed of Geraniums, Lilies and Cornflowers in the shape of an Anchor and inscribed thus, "This Anchor is laid here by the Coxswain and crew of the Spurn Lifeboat in loving memory of the men of Bradford who fell in the Great War".

Following this tribute of brave men to others, a hurried 'Sail' (As one of the men described it) was made in a fleet of motor cars to Wharfedale. The crew first called on the aged Mother of the branch secretary, (Mrs. Grainger) who, for many years has been an ardent lifeboat worker. The party then moved on to Rawdon where Mr. and Mrs. W. C. Gaunt extended a hearty welcome. Yeadon Vicarage was next visited and then Otley, where the stalwart men of Spurn were warmly cheered and were then addressed by Sir Hastings and Lady Duncan.

Birley was the next stop where a call was made to Mrs. J. G. Hutchinson, then on to Ilkley and the last stop on the tour. Here a very cordial welcome was extended by Miss Firth and the District Committee.

Returning to Bradford, the crew became the guests of the RNLI's old friend, Mr. Francis Laidler, at the Alhambra where they thoroughly enjoyed an entertainment which was greatly enhanced by the warmth of the real Yorkshire welcome extended to them.

At last the great day arrived, and there was the anxiety to see that the Kapok lifebelts were adjusted to a nicety, that the Medals were in a proper position and then to take up the position as Guard of Honour to the RNLI President, HRH The Prince of Wales on the occasion of his first visit to Bradford.

Then the order came, "Two deep - March" and so on into the City Square to take up their duties.

The Chairman of the Branch, Sir William Priestley, presented Coxswain Robert Cross to the Prince and the Coxswain in turn presented each member of his crew.

What keen interest, cheery enquiries and hearty good wishes come from the Royal Visitor. How kindly and sympathetically he referred to the RNLI's great work, how, generally 'bucked up' by his hearty handgrip and pleasant smile all the men are, and how delighted the Prince is to receive from Coxswain Cross the little medal lifeboat pin cushion with a 'Thank you very much Coxswain".

Back to the Hotel, each man cheered beyond measure by the princely nature of their reception, and so to the station in the presence of a large crowd for the return to Spurn where a man's work awaits them.

It was a visit that will long live in their memories of a fine crew with a remembrance of a real good time from the whole hearted Bradfordians. A knowledge that as soon as possible the 'City of Bradford' motor lifeboat will be stationed at Spurn Point and a feeling that the work of the lifeboat is very close to the heart of Bradford people".

The only other recorded rescue involving the lifeboat 'Samuel Oakes' took place on December 6th 1922, when the lifeboat was launched to go to the aid of a schooner later identified as the 'Hosanna' of Thurso. Coxswain Cross and his men aboard the 'Samuel Oakes' rescued the crew of 5 and returned them to the safety of the shore then put out again and saved the schooner. For their work in salvaging the abandoned vessel, the lifeboat crew were awarded salvage money and from his share of the award, Coxswain Cross sent the RNLI a donation of £2-5 shillings.

The Spurn lifeboat in November 1923 put in an appearance at the Naval Review at Spithead. In November 1923, a special review of the Atlantic Fleet was held at Spithead for the Dominion Prime Ministers then attending the Imperial Conference. On the day on which the review took place - a day of rough weather - the 'City of Bradford', the new motor lifeboat just handed over to the Spurn Station, which was built out of special funds raised in Bradford, was carrying out her sea trials and her appearance among the mighty ships of the Atlantic fleet was described in the Yorkshire Evening Post:-

"In the morning, as the 'Princess Margaret' slowly steamed down the line of ships, there appeared on the starboard side a motor lifeboat. Her oilskinned crew swept repeatedly by the dancing seas, the craft itself being almost smothered by the exuberant waters. Eventually, I made out her name, it was the Spurn lifeboat and on her side was painted the name 'City of Bradford',

It is well that the people of the northern City who brought her into being should know that their lifeboat is not afraid of the tempest."

CHAPTER SIX

RESCUES

Two services took place on the same day, November 25th 1925, and were to the same vessel, the SS 'Whinstone' of Preston, on her way from Hull to Berwick. Just before 8am that morning the Donna Nook lifeboat went out to aid in conditions which could have hardly been worse. A whole gale was blowing from the north, a tremendous sea was running and there were heavy squalls of snow. She pulled within hail of the vessel but found that, though she wanted the assistance of a tug, she was not at the moment in need of the lifeboat's help. The lifeboat therefore returned to her station, but the Hon. Secretary kept the 'Whinstone' under observation as he was confident that she would need help sooner or later and he advised the Spurn Lifeboat to stand by. His own crew were ready to put out again but they were so exhausted that he would not let them go.

The Humber lifeboat 'City of Bradford' was launched at 9.30am and she found the 'Whinstone' at anchor, after having run aground on the sands and the seas were breaking over her. By means of the Breeches buoy, the 6 men of her crew were hauled into the lifeboat. The lifeboat herself was buried in the breaking seas nearly all the time, and the Cox reported that it was the worst weather that he had ever known during 23 years in the lifeboat service.

In recognition of the skill and courage shown by both

The steam trawler 'Bengal' - Malcolm Fussey Photography.

crews in weather of such exceptional severity, the RNLI awarded to Coxswain Robert Cross of the Humber Lifeboat Station at Spurn, a Bar to his Silver Medal and to Coxswain John T. Dobson of Donna Nook the Bronze Medal. The RNLI also awarded the thanks of the Institution inscribed on Vellum to the second Coxswain and Bowman of Donna Nook and the Coxswains and crews of both lifeboats received extra monetary awards.

The Silver Medal which Coxswain Cross already held was awarded to him in December 1915 for his personal gallantry in jumping overboard from the lifeboat in the breaking water on a sandbank in order to get a line aboard a stranded ship.

He also held the Bronze Medal for a gallant attempt to rescue the crew of an unknown ship in October 1922, all the members of the crew on that occasion receiving the thanks of the Institution inscribed on Vellum.

On December 18th 1929, the Humber lifeboat 'City of Bradford II' was called out to the assistance of the steam trawler 'Bengal' which had gone aground during thick weather with a light W.N.W. breeze at Holmpton near Withernsea while returning from the fishing grounds. The lifeboat was launched at 3.45am and stayed with the trawler until the tide fell, then as her service were no longer required, she returned to her station arriving at 10am.

The 'Bengal' had stranded on the previous night and her crew had been rescued from the shore by the lifesaving apparatus. Later, they had returned to the trawler and while the lifeboat stood by, an unsuccessful attempt was made by the crew to refloat her. Permanent crew. Property salvage case.

On August 23rd 1930 the 'City of Bradford II' was launched at 3.40pm in a strong E.S.E. breeze with a rough sea and heavy rain to effect a rescue of the auxiliary Sloop 'Dakar' of Hull which was loading gravel on the south end of the Inner Binks but had got into severe difficulties when overcome by the incoming tide. The Sloop was swept and buried by heavy seas and the lifeboat, after getting as near as possible, effected communication by means of her line-throwing gun. The 'Dakar' then passed a hawser to the lifeboat and by this means she was gradually towed clear of the beach. The lifeboat still remained in attendance until it was ascertained that the Sloop had sustained no damage. The 'Dakar' then made for Grimsby under her own power and the lifeboat returned to her station arriving there at 4.30pm.

The owner of the 'Dakar', Mr. F. Burn of Beverley, sent a contribution of £5 to the RNLI in appreciation of the services rendered.

Permanent crew expenses, 7s.

On March 7th 1931 the Humber lifeboat 'City of Bradford II' was launched at 11.30pm in a rough sea with a strong easterly wind and snow showers, in response to distress signals fired by the Bull light vessel to indicate that an accident had occured in the vicinity. The lifeboat found the pilot cutter playing her searchlight on a vessel the SS 'Tern' of London. The cutter had taken off the crew of 15 of the 'Tern' which was in sinking condition following a collision with the SS 'City of Malines' while bound, laden from Hull to London. As the damaged vessel was a danger to navigation the lifeboat remained with her until, at 2.45am, she sank. Bearings of the wreck were taken and then the lifeboat returned ashore with the Captain and mate of the 'Tern' who had been transferred from the pilot cutter. The lifeboat arrived at her station at 7am.

Permanent crew expenses, 13/-.

On May 29th 1931 the Humber Lifeboat was launched at 9.45pm in a light S. breeze with a moderate sea, as the watchman on duty had reported flares at the mouth of the Humber and a rocket from the Spurn light vessel. Proceeding in the direction of the light vessel, the 'City of Bradford' found the Swedish motor fishing vessel 'Ella' of Ockero with a crew of 5 aboard. She had burst her petrol tank and her pumps were not working. A trawler was taking the 'Ella' in tow and the lifeboat remained with her until the disabled vessel was safely docked in Grimsby.

Permanent crew, expenses £1 14s.

On June 14th 1931 the Humber Lifeboat put out at 2.45pm in a moderate S.E. wind with a very rough sea, as a small motor fishing boat, the 'Felix' of Hull with a crew of 2, was in difficulties to the north of the Binks. She had made several unsuccessful attempts to cross them. As the lifeboat approached, the 'Felix' made another successful effort and the lifeboat escorted her into smooth water before returning to her station.

Permanent crew, expenses 13s.

One would imagine that boredom would be an everlasting problem with a full time crew of lifeboatmen at Spurn. Apart from the very necessary practices which were carried out at regular intervals, and the routine upkeep of the lifeboat and fittings together with general duties associated with the efficiency of the station, one would assume that the remoteness and the wind swept terrain, especially in winter, would allow time to drag on the crew. Presumably, in the early days, models would be made, letters would be written to lonely families, the general comradeship among the men would wear a bit thin after some weeks of inactivity. The Coxswain, therefore, would have to keep the peace and try to ensure harmony and good will during those days of rest.

Today, with television, radio and all modern conveniences, it is still possible to get bored, and the Spurn crew, I suppose are no exception. Men want action, and the sort of action at a lonely lifeboat station means going to someone's assistance. The trials and practices are routine but they don't concentrate the mind like a challenge presented by a vessel in trouble when the skills of the Coxswain and the courage of the crew are to be tested to the extreme.

However, at 9am on January 27th 1932 the lifeboat motor mechanic and the bowman put out in the boarding dinghy to start and run the lifeboat's engines and hang out riding lights. As they were rowing out to the moorings, a dense fog settled. They missed the lifeboat and drifted out to sea. After a time, anxiety was felt for their safety and the remainder of the lifeboat crew, thinking that they might have landed, searched the beach but without result. The motor lifeboat 'City of Bradford I' was then launched and went in the direction of the Binks, searched the coast for about 7 miles to the north and returned on a zig zag course, still without avail.

Inquiry was made at the Royal Naval signal station by semaphore where it learned that the men had not been seen and that there had been a collision 21 miles N. by E. of Spurn. It was now 2.30pm and the fog was lifting. The lifeboat made for the Spurn light vessel, and just as they arrived, a steam trawler was seen making for the Humber with the lifeboat's dinghy in tow, she had picked the men up 8 miles north of the light vessel.

After taking the 2 men aboard, the Coxswain made for the scene of the collision, but there was nothing to be seen, and after cruising around for some time the lifeboat returned to her station, arriving back at 8.30pm. It was later learned that the SS 'Larchwood' and SS 'Burma' had been in collision without loss of life.

Permanent crew.

(Authors Note, It would seem that from 1929 to 1932 there were two lifeboats stationed at Spurn, the City of Bradford I and II. The No.II lifeboat served as the emergency lifeboat until December 1932).

We must remember that from 1924 the station was known as the Humber Lifeboat Station although to many diehards the name will always be 'SPURN'.

At 6.10pm on 18th September 1932 one of the lifeboat crew reported to the Coxswain that a small yacht, the 'Thrush' of Hull, had stranded on the end of Spurn Point. A light N.W. breeze was blowing and at their request the motor lifeboat 'City of BradfordII' put out and towed the 'Thrush' to a safe anchorage in Spurn Gut.

Permanent crew.

On 13th January 1933 at 8.47pm, the Royal Naval signal station reported that a vessel was ashore $1\frac{1}{2}$ miles north east of the station. The motor lifeboat 'City of Bradford No.1' was launched and proceeded to the scene. The vessel in trouble was the steam trawler 'Tranio' of Hull. She had stranded while bound laden from the Faroes to Hull carrying a crew of 13. A light variable wind was blowing with a slight ground swell, but a dense fog had settled. The lifeboat stood by at the request of the skipper, and later ran out a kedge anchor to be picked up by the tugs which had been sent for. Owing to the fog, the tugs were not able to find the trawler, but she refloated on the flood tide and went on her way to Hull. The lifeboat then returned to her station and arrived back at 7am. She had been on service for 10 hours.

Property salvage case.

The very next day, January 14th 1933, the Spanish steamer 'Arantzazu' of Bilbao stranded 6 miles south of Haile buoy while bound laden from Bilbao to Immingham. She carried a crew of 29, and wirelessed for help and the motor lifeboat 'City of Bradford No.1' was launched at 11.45pm. A strong and increasing S.S.W. breeze was blowing with a rough sea and patches of fog. The lifeboat stood by the 'Arantzazu' and at the request of her Master, ran out a kedge anchor. This enabled her to refloat on the flood tide, then the lifeboat escorted her up the Humber to safety. The lifeboat was out for over 9 hours and returned to her station at 9am.

Property salvage case.

On April 1st 1933 the 'City of Bradford No.1' was called out at 11pm after the lifeboat watchman had reported that a vessel had run aground on the Inner Binks. A N.W. to W. wind was blowing, with a rough ground sea. The 'City of Bradford No.1' found the steam trawler 'Lord Harewood' of Grimsby, rolling heavily and thumping on the bottom. She was bound, laden, with a crew of 12, from the fishing grounds to Grimsby.

The lifeboat dropped anchor and stood by until daybreak. She then passed tow ropes from the trawler to a tug that had arrived to refloat her. After the tug had pulled for half an hour, the tow parted and this left the 'Lord Harewood' in a very dangerous position. The lifeboat, however, managed to pass another hawser between the two vessels and eventually the trawler was refloated. Her skipper was very grateful for the lifeboat's help. The lifeboat arrived back at her station at 7.30am, having been on service for over 8 hours.

Property salvage case.

Several small yachts visited Spurn on the 9th July 1933. After they had set out again, a heavy squall sprang up and one of the yachts - the 'Alice' of Grimsby - drifted aground on the Trinity Sands. A strong squally breeze was blowing with a short choppy sea and it was raining hard. The 'Alice' was seen from the lifeboat station and the motor lifeboat 'City of Bradford I' was launched at 4pm. She found that the 3 men on board the 'Alice' had got onto the Trinity Sand bank which was entirely surrounded by water.

The 'Alice' was towed off, and the men were taken off by an Easington coble that was fishing nearby and the men were transferred to the lifeboat. The men and their boat were then taken to Grimsby by the lifeboat which returned to her station at 7.30pm.

Permanent crew, rewards 6/-.

On 13th October 1933 the Spurn Royal Naval signal station reported to the Coxswain that the Holmpton Coastguard had reported a steam trawler ashore at Dimlington. She was the 'Kirby' of Grimsby, bound home from the fishing grounds with a crew of 12. The motor lifeboat 'City of Bradford No.1' was launched at 6.30am, but found it impossible to get near the 'Kirby' at once, owing to the shallow water and the heavy ground sea breaking outside her. When the tide flowed the lifeboat anchored and veered down through the broken water to the trawler. She then took out an anchor, which kept her from washing farther ashore.

Later a tug arrived with a representative of the owners on board, and at his request the lifeboat connected the tug to the trawler. With the assistance of the tug, the 'Kirby' was refloated and then the lifeboat returned to her station arriving back at 3pm.

Property salvage case.

On 14th October, just enough time to allow the crew of the lifeboat to get their breath back, they were called out to a trawler stranded in foggy weather. The lifeboat was launched and went to assist but the trawler, which was not identified, had refloated and continued on her way.

Permanent crew, rewards 18/-.

On the evening of 15th December 1933 the steam trawler 'Thanet' was seen to run aground on the Inner Binks sands. She carried a crew of 9 and was returning home from the fishing grounds. The motor lifeboat 'City of Bradford II' was launched at 7.45pm in a light E. wind adn with a moderate sea, and found the 'Thanet' lying in a very awkward position. She ran out the trawler's anchor and returned ashore to report to her owners. Then, at their request, she went back to the 'Thanet' and stood by until

The steam trawler 'Thanet' - Malcolm Fussey Photography.

she refloated at 12.20am, on the 16th. She had not been damaged by the grounding and went on her way. The lifeboat arrived back at her station at 1am.

Property salvage case.

On 21st December 1933 a vessel ran aground on the Binks in thick fog, the lifeboat was launched but the vessel was seen to have found deep water and was observed to be continuing on her voyage.

Permanent crew, rewards £1 7/-.

On 31st January 1934 a hulk without lights had broken away from her tug off Chapel St. Leonards, thirty five miles from the Humber Lifeboat Station and it was believed that a man was on board. The sea was heavy with a strong northerly wind and rain. After searching throughout the night without success, the lifeboat returned at 10am having been at sea for 12 hours. It was learned later that there had been no one aboard the hulk. In appreciation of this long and arduous search, a special monetary award was made to each of the lifeboat crew.

Permanent crew, rewards £5-0s-3d.

At five minutes past nine on 2nd March 1934 the lifeboat watchman reported that a Steamer had drifted ashore on the Inner Binks. She was in a dangerous position, and the motor lifeboat 'City of Bradford No.1' was launched. A light but freshening S.W. breeze was blowing and the weather was misty. The lifeboat found that the vessel was the SS 'Monarch' of Glasgow bound from London to the Humber for orders. Her Captain said that he would signal at flood tide if he wanted any help, so the lifeboat stood by. The Steamer refloated, unaided, on the flood tide and the lifeboat then returned to her station arriving at 4.30am.

Permanent crew, rewards 18/-.

The Humber Lifeboat 'City of Bradford No.1' was called out at noon on 3rd April 1934 as the Spurn Royal Naval signal station reported that a steamer appeared to be unmanageable. Later, she ran aground on Spurn Point. She was the SS 'Lancashire' of Sunderland laden with a cargo of pit props bound to Dover from Sunderland and carrying a crew of 8 men and 2 women passengers. The sea was moderate with a strong N.E. breeze.

The 'City of Bradford No.1' was launched and took off the 2 women and then stood by. As the tide ebbed there was a great danger that the 'Lancashire' would roll over into deep water so the lifeboat took off the crew and returned to her station.

On the flood tide, the crew were taken back to their ship and the 'City of Bradford' stood by her until she refloated and had safely anchored. The women were then taken back to the 'Lancashire' and the lifeboat finally returned to her station at 7pm.

The Underwriters sent a gift of money to the lifeboat crew in appreciation of their services.

Permanent crew, rewards 6/-.

Early on the morning of May 17th 1934, the lifeboat watchman heard a vessel sounding SOS on her siren, and a little later the Spurn Royal Naval signal station telephoned that a trawler was aground near Kilnsea beacon. She was the steam trawler 'Salacon' of Grimsby bound home from the fishing grounds with a crew of 11. The motor lifeboat 'City of Bradford No.1' was launched at 3.45am in a fresh to strong W.N.W. breeze with a heavy ground sea.

She found the trawler had already dropped one anchor and at the request of the skipper the lifeboat laid out another. Then, as the crew of the trawler did not wish to leave her, the 'City of Bradford' stood by. With the flowing tide the trawler was driven inshore before the sea, but when the tide ebbed out she was out of danger. The lifeboat then returned to her station arriving there at 10.30am.

Property salvage case.

However, 4 days later the Spurn lifeboat was called out to assist a motor boat 'The Withernsea Monster'. The 'City of Bradford No.1' was launched at 1.10pm on May 21st 1934 as a report in the form of a telephone call from the Withernsea Coastguard that the 'Withernsea Monster' had broken down and was drifting five miles east of the Coastguard Station.

The lifeboat found that the motorboat had already been towed home by the motor fishing boat 'Melba' of Grimsby so the lifeboat returned to her station at 4.45pm.

A few minutes later another message was received from Withernsea that 2 men in a rowing boat appeared to be in trouble. A squally W.N.W. breeze was blowing and the sea was smooth. Luckily, the lifeboat was launched again at 5.15pm and found the rowing boat 'Ivy' of Tunstall riding at anchor about 1 mile off Tunstall. The boat had no sails and the men were exhausted after trying to row her in. The lifeboat towed them to safety and returned to her station again at 9.15pm.

Permanent crew, rewards 6/- and 15/-.

A slightly different rescue was effected on 24th August 1934 when a man was cut off on the sands by the tide, in spite of the lifeboat's presence. The man managed to get ashore without their help.

Permanent crew, rewards 6/-.

Early in the morning of 8th September 1934 the lifeboat watchman saw rockets in the direction of Kilnsea and the motor lifeboat 'City of Bradford No.1' was launched at 5am. A moderate S.S.E. breeze was blowing with a moderate sea and the weather was misty. The lifeboat found the Danish motor fishing vessel 'Noordstjernan' of Frederickshaven ashore $2\frac{1}{2}$ miles north of the Lifeboat Station.

She carried a crew of 4 and was returning from the fishing grounds. At the request of her skipper the lifeboat ran out an anchor and stood by her until after high water. The lifeboat returned to her station, getting back at 7.45am. The fishing vessel was later towed off by a tug and was taken into the Humber.

Permanent crew, rewards 9/-.

On the afternoon of September 19th 1934 the pleasure boat 'Sunbeam' of Cleethorpes took a party of 14 to Spurn. Shortly after she had left on the return journey the signal station watchman reported that she seemed to be in difficulties and the motor lifeboat 'City of Bradford No.1' was launched and hastened to her assistance at 5pm. A strong S.W. breeze was blowing and the sea was very choppy.

The 'Sunbeam' was seen to be lying broadside on to the swell and in the full strength of the tide, she was shipping water and all the people on board were soaking wet. The lifeboat ran alongside and took off 13 of the 14 aboard, then a rope was passed to the remaining man and the 'Sunbeam' was towed back to Cleethorpes. The lifeboat arrived back at her station at 6.45pm.

Permanent crew, rewards 6/-.

At 1.10am on the 24th November 1934 the Spurn Point Royal Naval signal station reported that a vessel was aground 1 mile north of Kilnsea. The sea was smooth, but a fog had come down and it was decided to send out the motor lifeboat 'City of Bradford II'. (No.1 had since been withdrawn and put into the pool of reserve lifeboats). She left at 1.45am and, searching the area northwards found the steam trawler 'Chrysea' of Grimsby, aground $^1/_2$ a mile north of Easington. She carried a crew of 10 and was returning from the fishing grounds. The lifeboat offered help but the skipper said that he would first try to get the trawler off himself. A ground swell was now making, and the trawler's small boat, which had been launched, was smashed against her as she rolled. The lifeboat stood by until 4.15am when the 'Chrysea' refloated and went on her way towards Grimsby. The lifeboat returned to her station at 5am.

Permanent crew, rewards 9/-.

On 10th November 1934, a barge was known to have gone ashore but the lifeboat could not find her in the darkness as she had not shown lights. The barge remained ashore, but her crew were in no danger.

Permanent crew, rewards £1-2s-6d.

On November 22nd 1934, a motor vessel became stranded but a tug was in the area and gave the help needed.

Permanent crew, rewards 9/-.

On the evening of 22nd January 1935 the Royal Naval shore signal station telephoned that a vessel about the size of a trawler appeared to have run aground on Spurn Point, south of the Military Pier. Two of the lifeboat crew went to investigate and reported that a trawler was ashore at a place where the beach had a steep slope. The motor lifeboat 'City of Bradford II' was launched at 9-5pm. A

light wind was blowing and the sea was smooth. The lifeboat found the trawler to be the 'Harvardour IS-FIRDINGUR' of Isafjordur bound from Grimsby to the fishing grounds. She carried a crew of 16. Shortly after the lifeboat got alongside, the trawler gave a list to port. Her crew were afraid that she would capsize and asked at first to be taken off. They stayed, however, and the lifeboat stood by. At low water the lifeboat ran out an anchor which was hove in tight on the trawler's winch and about 7am the next morning the trawler hauled herself off and put to sea. The lifeboat returned to her station at 8am having been at sea on service for 10 hours.

Property salvage case.

On 8th July 1935 a small boat had been stolen from Cleethorpes and with 3 people on board, the boat was drifting out to sea. The lifeboat was launched and the boat was found and the lifeboat recalled.

Permanent crew, rewards 6/-.

On the evening of the 12th October 1935 a message was received from a contractor that one of his men who was working on the Bull Fort, in the River Humber, had been taken seriously ill, and that it was necessary to get him to Grimsby Hospital as soon as possible. The motor lifeboat 'City of Bradford II' was launched at 6.45pm, took the man from the Bull Fort then to Grimsby where an ambulance was waiting to take him to Hospital. The lifeboat returned to her station at 8pm. The contractor made a donation to the RNLI and another to the lifeboat crew.

Permanent crew, rewards 18/-.

On the 19th October 1935 the SS 'Magrix' of Hull was at anchor off Spurn in a whole W. gale, with a rough sea. At 11.40am she began to drift and went ashore on the Point. She was on a dead lee shore with the seas breaking over her. The motor lifeboat 'City of Bradford II' was launched, she went to the vessel, anchored and veered down, but the Captain of the 'Magrix' decided that he and his crew would remain on board. The lifeboat stood by and as the tide ebbed, the crew were able to walk ashore. Owing to the gale; it was impossible to rehouse the 'City of Bradford' at her station, so she spent the night in the Royal Dock Basin at Grimsby and returned to Spurn the next morning.

Permanent crew, rewards £2-5-3d.

At about 10pm on November 18th 1935 the Coxswain, Robert Cross, saw that the Middle Gas Float had broken from its moorings and was drifting out of the Humber, becoming a danger to navigation. The sea was smooth, with a light southerly wind, and the tide was ebbing. A small boat was manned by the lifeboat crew and the float was intercepted and moored near the Inner Binks buoy.

When the matter was reported to the Humber Conservancy Board, the Board requested that the float should be brought in on the flood tide, and at 4.45am the motor lifeboat 'City of Bradford II' was launched. She went to the float, placed 2 men on board and came in with it on the flood, eventually mooring it inside Spurn. Later the float was taken in tow by a tug and the lifeboat returned to her Station at 6.45am. The Humber Conservancy Board made a gift to the lifeboat crew in appreciation of their services.

Permanent crew.

On the morning of November 25th 1935 it was reported that a steamer was apparently aground near the Inner Binks and the motor lifeboat 'City of Bradford II' was launched at 10.15am. The wind was only light with a slight ground swell, but it was foggy. The lifeboat found the Swedish steamer 'Groveland' of Raa, hard aground between the Inner Binks and Spurn Lighthouse. The lifeboat stood by her until 1pm as the 'Groveland' floated clear on the flood tide, then, acting on the Coxswain's advice and following the lead given by the lifeboat, the 'Groveland' got safely into the Channel and, after thanking the lifeboat's crew for their help, went up the Humber.

The lifeboat returned to her Station at 2pm.

Property salvage case.

On 20th December 1935 sounds of guns being fired called the Spurn lifeboat out to find the cause, but no trace of vessels could be found so lifeboat returned to her Station.

Permanent crew, rewards 9/-.

On 24th January 1936 it was reported that a vessel had grounded, but when the lifeboat was launched to investigate it was found she was anchored close inshore and not in any danger.

Permanent crew, rewards 9/-.

Early on the morning of 17th February 1936, the Mablethorpe Coastguard reported a vessel ashore at Saltfleet Haven. A moderate S.E. breeze was blowing with a moderate ground swell.

The motor lifeboat 'City of Bradford II' was launched at 6am and proceeded to the scene. She found the motor barge 'River Witham' of Hull stranded on the beach. The lifeboat stood by in case her help was needed, but the 'River Witham' was washed high up the beach by the flood tide. The lifeboat then returned to her Station at 12.30pm.

Permanent paid crew, rewards £1-0s-3d.

At 6.20am on 23rd February 1936 it was learned from the Spurn Royal Naval signal station that the trawler 'Algorma' of Grimsby was ashore 9 miles north of Spurn, and in need of help. The wind was light, but there was a heavy sea. The motor lifeboat 'City of Bradford II' was launched at 6.45am and found the 'Algorma' ashore close under Dimlington Cliff.

She was anchored and veered in. The 'Algorma' was practically dry forward and as the Board of Trade lifesaving rocket apparatus had got a line on board, her crew decided to go ashore in the breeches-Buoy. The lifeboat stood by while this was being done, and returned to her Station at 10.50am.

The crew of the 'Algorma' later returned to their ship and she refloated on the following tide.

Permanent crew, rewards £1-0s-3d.

Just before noon on May 31st 1936, a small fishing boat 'The Lily' of Grimsby drifted ashore inside Spurn Point. She was in no immediate danger, a moderate N.N.W. breeze was blowing with a slight swell.

Later on the Royal Naval signal station reported that the crew of 'The Lily' appeared to be signalling for help and the motor lifeboat 'City of Bradford II' was launched at 1pm. She found 'The Lily' in a helpless condition, her anchors had been lost, her propellor had been fouled and her crew were exhausted. The lifeboat got a tow rope on board and towed 'The Lily' into Grimsby. The lifeboat returned to her Station at 3.20pm.

Permanent paid crew.

On the morning of 18th August 1936 a trawler was seen to be aground on the Middle Binks. She was the 'Runswick Bay' of Hull, bound for the fishing grounds and she carried a crew of 15. A light breeze was blowing and the sea was smooth, but as the trawler was near a sunken wreck, the lifeboat 'City of Bradford II' was launched at noon. She ran out an anchor for the trawler and then stood by. At half flood tide the 'Runswick Bay' heaved on the anchor and eventually floated clear. The lifeboat crew made a donation to the RNLI from the money received for their salvage services.

Property salvage case.

In the morning of November 12th 1936 the ever vigilant lifeboat watchman saw a small vessel flying a signal and drifting slowly towards the Binks. A moderate S.E. breeze was blowing with a nasty sea. The motor lifeboat 'City of Bradford II' was launched at 9.30am and found the motor fishing vessel 'Aud Schou' of Frederick-shaven, Denmark at anchor near the Binks, she had dropped anchor just before the 'City of Bradford' arrived as her engine had broken down and her Skipper asked to be towed out of danger. The lifeboat towed the 'Aud Schou' to Grimsby and returned to her Station at 2pm.

Property salvage case.

On 15th January 1937 distress rockets were reported seen coming from a vessel north of Mablethorpe. The 'City of Bradford II' had been launched and searched the area but nothing was found.

Rewards. 13s-6d. Permanent paid crew.

On the morning of the 29th January 1937, the Spurn Point Royal Naval signal station telephoned that the Steamer 'Edmond Hugo Stinnes' of Hamburg had sent out a wireless message that she was in distress with a broken rudder about 35 miles N.E. of the Humber. A whole E. gale was blowing with heavy squalls of snow and hail. The motor lifeboat 'City of Bradford II' was launched at 8.35am, she could not find any trace of the Steamer, but at 3pm radioed a tug which had also answered the call for assistance. As the lifeboat had not

sufficient petrol on board to continue to search all night, she made her station, arriving at 8.35pm. She had been 12 hours at sea under very bad conditions, being continuously swept by the the heavy seas. It was afterwards learnt that the 'Edmond Hugo Stinnes' had gone on her way. A special money award was paid to the members of the crew and the owners of the 'Edmond Hugo Stinnes' sent a letter of thanks and paid a donation to the RNLI.

Rewards £7-0s-3d. Permanent paid crew.

At about 4.35am on 21st February 1937, the Spurn lifeboat watchman reported that a vessel had run ashore about $\frac{1}{4}$ mile N. of Spurn light vessel. She was the steam trawler 'Rose of England' of Grimsby, bound for the fishing grounds.

She had been in collision with another trawler and had been badly holed.

Five of her crew of 10 had been taken off by a third trawler and the remaining 5 of the crew had run her aground to stop her sinking. These men were still aboard. A strong W.N.W. breeze was blowing with a nasty ground sea and it was thought at first that the 'Rose of England' could be approached along the shore but this was found to be impossible and the motor lifeboat 'City of Bradford II' was launched at 5.45am. When she arrived the trawler's decks were awash. She rescued the 5 men and took them to Grimsby returning to her Station at 12.50pm.

Rewards £1-0s-3d. Permanent paid crew.

On 6th April 1937 at 7.38pm the Donna Nook Coastguard reported that a vessel was ashore north of the Donna Nook beacon. A gentle breeze was blowing, with a slight swell but dense fog persisted. The motor lifeboat 'City of Bradford II' was launched at 8.15pm and feeling her way through the fog, found the Hull trawler 'Sir John Lister' hard aground on the Haile Sand with her head to the sea. The lifeboat stood by and later ran out an anchor from the trawler. The trawler then heaved on it with her winch and hauled herself off into deep water. Owing to the dense fog, the Skipper decided to remain at anchor, and as the trawler was no longer in danger, the lifeboat made for her Station arriving at 1.30am on the 7th.

Permanent crew. Property salvage case.

The motor lifeboat 'City of Bradford II' was launched at 10.30am on May 11th 1937 in response to a message received from the Humber Conservancy that a vessel had collided with the Bull Light vessel during a fog. The sea was moderate with a fresh E.N.E. wind blowing.

The lifeboat found that the light vessel had been damaged but above the water line and she returned and reported to the Conservancy Board.

Permanent paid crew.

On 14th April 1937 two steamers had been in collision twenty miles from Spurn but could not be found by the Spurn lifeboat owing to dense fog. One foundered, her crew being rescued by a nearby steamer, and the other, although taking water, reached the Humber.

Permanent crew, rewards 9s.

On 29th April 1937, a steamer reported by wireless that she had been in collision with the Bull Lightship but the lifeboat found upon investigation that the lightship did not need any assistance.

Permanent paid crew.

During the afternoon of 27th August 1937 the Mablethorpe Coastguard reported through Spurn Point signal station that two trawlers had been in collision ten miles north of the Humber and that one of them was sinking. They were the 'Polly Johnson' of Hull and the Scarron of Grimsby, both bound for the fishing grounds. The breeze was light and the sea smooth when the motor lifeboat 'City of Bradford II' was launched at 3.20pm. She sighted the trawlers about 15 miles north and spoke to the 'Polly Johnson'. She was badly damaged but was able to get back to the Humber without help.

The lifeboat then went to the 'Scarron' which was very extensively damaged and apparently sinking. The Skipper said that the bulkhead was holding and that all his pumps were working.

An injured man was then transferred to the lifeboat and she stood by in company with another trawler which had arrived. At 8pm a tug arrived with representatives of the owners on board. They asked the lifeboat to escort the 'Scarron' into the Humber as she was likely to sink at any minute. The lifeboat did so as far as the Bull Lightship where another tug arrived and the 'Scarron' was taken in

tow stern first. The lifeboat went into Grimsby where the injured man was landed and taken to hospital. The lifeboat then returned to her Station arriving at 3am on the 28th.

Permanent paid crew, rewards 9s.

At about 3.40am on 30th August 1937 the eagle eyed watchman at Spurn reported a vessel ashore on the Inner Binks, but not in immediate danger. A light breeze was blowing with a smooth sea. The motor lifeboat 'City of Bradford II' was launched at 4.35am in case her help should be needed and subsequently found the vessel to be the motor fishing vessel 'Sophie' of Frederickshaven, bound for Grimsby from the fishing grounds. The lifeboat stood by and when the tide flowed and there was enough water for her to get alongside the 'Sophie', she ran out an anchor for her. A line was then passed from the 'Sophie' to the lifeboat which held on tight to it until the 'Sophie' had hauled herself off into deep water. The 'Sophie' went on her way and the lifeboat made for her Station arriving at 9.45am.

Property salvage case.

During the afternoon of 31st August 1937 the motor yacht 'Sea Hawk' ran ground in a very dangerous position some 3 miles from the north east point of Spurn. She was bound for home from Bridlington with 3 men on board, one of whom got ashore in a small boat and went to the lifeboat station for help. The lifeboat crew went along the shore and found the 'Sea Hawk' high and dry and at the Coxswain's suggestion an anchor was run out to prevent her washing up the beach when the tide flowed and the lifeboat returned to their station leaving 2 men to help the yacht's crew.

The wind freshened and at 10.45pm a moderate S.E. breeze was blowing with a nasty swell, and the night was very dark with intermittent rain.

The motor lifeboat 'City of Bradford II' was launched and signalled to the lifeboat men on the yacht to stand on near the nearby groynes and shine their torches. By their light the lifeboat was taken in between the groynes and a line was fired ashore. By this means a rope was passed to the yacht.

As the tide flowed the lifeboat, helped by the men on

the 'Sea Hawk', hauled the yacht clear and she was towed to Grimsby. The lifeboat returned to her Station arriving at 4.30am on September 1st.

Property salvage case.

Previously, on August 29th 1937, two steamers had collided. One sank but her crew were rescued by the other vessel. The lifeboat could not do very much to help in this case.

Permanent paid crew, rewards 9/-.

During a dense fog on the morning of October 3rd 1937, the Spurn Point Royal Naval shore signal station reported an unknown vessel ashore near Kilnsea beacon. She was the Greek steamer 'Ais Giorgis' of Piraeus bound with a cargo of timber from the White Sea for Grimsby and Hull. She carried a crew of 21. The breeze was light but there was a swell on the beach. The motor lifeboat 'City of Bradford II' was launched at 8.45am and put 4 men on the steamer and then ran out an anchor for her. When the tide flowed, the 4 men hove on the steamer's winch and she refloated and went on her way. The lifeboat returned to her Station at 3pm.

Property salvage case.

At 8.35am, on the 20th October 1937, a request was received for the motor lifeboat 'City of Bradford II' to go to the Bull Fort in the mouth of the Humber to take a man to Hospital. A light W. breeze was blowing with a smooth sea and patchy fog.

The lifeboat was launched at 8.55am and proceeded to the Bull Fort where the sick man was lowered into the lifeboat and she made for Grimsby where an ambulance was waiting. The lifeboat then returned to her Station and arrived there at 11.45pm but was not rehoused until the tide flowed at 2.30am. The man's employers expressed their appreciation of the help given and made a donation to the RNLI to cover expenses.

No expense to RNLI.

At 1.50pm the following day, October 21st 1937, during a lift in the fog, a vessel was seen to run hard aground on the beach near the lifeboat house. The wind was light and the sea state slight. The motor lifeboat 'City of Bradford II' was launched at 2.10pm and found the vessel to be the steam trawler 'King's Grey' of Hull bound, with a crew of 14 for the fishing grounds. On the advice of Coxswain Cross, the 'King's Grey' dropped her bow anchor and then went astern on her engines. She refloated but the strong tide carried her back on the beach again. After further help from Coxswain Cross she got off the beach with an almighty effort and went on her way and the lifeboat returned to her Station, arriving there at 3.30pm.

Property salvage case.

On the 21st October 1937 at 10.45pm, the exhausted lifeboat crew found themselves called out again. The 'City of Bradford II' was launched as the lifeboat watchman reported that two maroons had been fired in the direction of the Bull Light vessel. A gentle S. breeze was blowing with a smooth sea but dense fog conditions made visibility very difficult. After groping about and with great difficulty, the lifeboat found the Bull Light vessel and went alongside. The Coxswain went on board and found that the light vessel had been struck by another vessel which had gone on her way. The Bull Light vessel's damage was to her starboard bow and she had broken away from her moorings. The lifeboat helped to get the broken mooring chain on board and stood by until it was found that the light vessel was sound and not taking in water. The 'City of Bradford' then made to return to her Station arriving at 3.15am.

Permanent paid crew, rewards 18/-.

On October 30th 1937, a steam fishing vessel had run aground at Easington but her crew had been rescued by the Coastguard's rocket saving equipment and the services of the lifeboat were not needed in this case. Nevertheless, the lifeboat was launched and she stood by for a while.

Permanent crew, rewards 18/-.

On December 13th 1937, the watchman at the Lifeboat Station reported that a vessel had run aground on the Trinity Sands. The time was 3am and the vessel appeared to be in in no immediate danger and the tide was ebbing. Later the S.S.E. breeze increased to gale and when the tide changed it was decided to launch the lifeboat. At 8.30am the lifeboat 'City of Bradford II' was launched and found the Hull trawler 'Almondine', bound for the fishing grounds with a crew of 10 hard aground. On the Coxswain's advice she dropped a bow anchor to prevent her drifting farther onto the sands and at 11am she refloated. The lifeboat then piloted her into deep water and she continued on her way. The lifeboat then returned to her Station.

Property salvage case.

At 7.45pm on December 17th 1937, the lifeboat watchman reported two rockets in a south-easterly direction. A strong N.W. breeze was blowing with a rough sea, squalls of rain and sleet. The motor lifeboat 'City of Bradford II' was launched at 8.15pm and was directed by Spurn Light vessel to the Humber Light vessel. Here she learned that one of the crew was in great pain with a poisoned hand and with some difficulty he was taken aboard the lifeboat which then headed for Grimsby. The man was landed in the Royal Dock Basin where an ambulance took him to Hospital. The lifeboat then returned to her Station arriving at 2.20am on 18th December.

Permanent paid crew, rewards 18/-.

On 31st December 1937, it was reported by the watchman that flares had been sighted coming from near the Inner Dowsing Light vessel. The lifeboat was launched and searched the area concerned, but no sign of a ship in distress was found. Failing the discovery of vessels in distress, the 'City of Bradford II' returned to her Station. It appeared that in this service the Skegness Lifeboat also took part, another example of neighbouring lifeboats helping each other in emergencies.

The Skegness Lifeboat, being a voluntary crew, was paid £19-14-6d. The Humber Lifeboat, having a full time paid crew, received the princely sum of £18.

At about 4.50pm on 12th February 1938, information was received through the Mablethorpe Coastguard and the Spurn Point Royal Naval Shore signal station that a vessel was drifting onto the Haile Sands. She was identified as the London registered steamer 'Deerwood' with a crew of 19 aboard. A whole gale was blowing from the North East with a heavy sea and squalls of rain and hail.

The motor lifeboat 'City of Bradford II' was launched

at 5.15pm and found that the 'Deerwood' had damaged her propellor. She was very near the Sands but was holding her own with both anchors down and her engines full ahead. Her Master had already sent for a tug and the lifeboat stood by until the tug arrived in case the crew had to be taken off. Shortly after 7pm the tug arrived and commenced towing the 'Deerwood' to Grimsby escorted by the lifeboat. On passing the Bull Light vessel, the lifeboat Coxswain learned the Light vessel had been driven from her moorings but that her spare anchor was holding and she did not need immediate assistance. The weather was so bad that the 'City of Bradford' could not be rehoused at her Station, so she ran for the berth in the Royal Dock Basin at Grimsby where she sheltered overnight, arriving at 10.15pm. She managed to return to Spurn on the following day and on her way back the Coxswain spoke to the 'Deerwood' whose Captain thanked the Coxswain and crew for their services.

Permanent crew, rewards £2-12-2d.

Two days later the Humber Lifeboat was in action again when just after 9pm on 14th February 1938 the watchman reported that a large steamer was aground on the Inner Binks. The sea was rough, with an E.N.E. wind and snow squalls. At 9.30pm the motor lifeboat 'City of Bradford II' was launched and found the steamer to be the London registered 'King Edgar', a steamer of 4,500 tons, laden with railway sleepers and bound from Vancouver to Immingham, Lincs. The Coxswain, Robert Cross, went aboard her and after discussion, it was decided that the lifeboat should stand by as tugs were on their way. At 2am, when the flood tide was at its strongets, the 'King Edgar' refloated, to everyone's relief, without help, and went on her way to Immingham. The lifeboat, then made her way back to her Station, arriving at 3am.

Property salvage case.

Shortly after midnight on March 19th 1938, the motor vessel 'Confid' of Rotterdam, bound laden from Plymouth for Middlesbrough, ran aground on the Inner Binks. A moderate south westerly breeze was blowing with a slight to moderate sea, Spurn Royal Naval Shore signal station and the lifeboat watchman reported the 'Confid' ashore and the motor lifeboat 'City of Bradford

II' was launched at 12.11am on the 20th. The lifeboat anchored and veered down but owing to the very shallow water she could not get alongside. There was a slight swell and the wind had started to freshen. The Coxswain decided to stand by until the 'Confid' could perhaps refloat, which she did at 4am. The lifeboat guided her to a safe anchorage inside Spurn Point and then returned to her Station, arriving at 5am.

Permanent paid crew, rewards 9/-.

At 6.40am on the 27th May 1938, the Spurn Signal Station reported that a vessel was drifting at sea. A light southerly wind was blowing at the time with a moderate sea running. The motor lifeboat 'City of Bradford II' was launched at 7.30am and found the fishing boat 'Young Dick' of Hull with only one man aboard. The boat was drifting towards the Middle Binks, her anchor having dragged while the man was asleep. The lifeboat ran alongside and put two men on board and brought the fishing boat into safety.

Permanent paid crew, rewards 6/-.

At 7.45am on the 7th August 1938, it was reported from Easington, through the Humber Signal Station, that a vessel was ashore at Dimlington Heights.

A moderate northerly breeze was blowing, with a moderate sea. There was also fog and rain, all in all not a very nice day! The motor lifeboat 'J. W. Archer', on temporary duties at Spurn while the 'City of BradfordII' was undergoing overhaul, put out at 8.20am and found the Grimsby trawler 'Capricornus', with a crew of 9 had stranded while returning to Grimsby from the fishing grounds. She was broadside on to the beach. The wind was increasing and a swell making, as the flood tide made, an anchor hawser fouled the bilge keel and the trawler became quite unmanageable. The lifeboat stood by and advised the Skipper what to do until the tug 'Lynx' arrived and was able to take the 'Capricornus' in tow to Grimsby. The lifeboat then returned to her Station arriving at 3pm.

Permanent paid crew, rewards 6/-.

On the 29th August 1938 at about 2.30am a message was received from the Donna Nook Coastguard that a vessel 5 miles S.S.E. was firing rockets. A fresh north-erly breeze was blowing with a rough sea, and the weather was thick with rain. The relief motor lifeboat 'J. W. Archer' was launched at 2.50am and found the SS 'Salerno' of Hull bound laden from Oslo for Hull ashore at Saltfleet. She was lying broadside on to the sea which was breaking into her but the lifeboat managed to get under her lee. At her Master's request, two lifeboatmen managed to go aboard the 'Salerno' and the lifeboat ran out an anchor for her. With the help of this anchor the 'Salerno' was refloated on the flood tide and she went on her way and the lifeboat returned to her Station arriving at 9.15am.

Property salvage case.

On October 10th 1939, the watchman at Spurn, at 4.20am, saw a vessel heading for the beach. He gave the alarm and the motor lifeboat 'City of Bradford II' was launched at 4.55am. A gale had been blowing, it had dropped to a fresh wind from the South-South West, but it had left a very heavy sea running. Twenty minutes after she launched the lifeboat found the steam trawler 'Saltaire' of Grimsby aground on the Inner Binks. She was rolling, her gunwales right under, and the seas were breaking over her. The trawler was lying head off shore, so the Coxswain anchored to windward and dropped down his cable. By the light of his searchlight he came alongside and held the lifeboat there while the 9 men of the trawler's crew jumped aboard. One of the men fell between the trawler and the lifeboat but he was pulled aboard before the seas had flung them together again. At 6.30am the rescued men were landed.

At low water it was possible to walk out to the 'Saltaire' and by now the wind had dropped. Her crew, with the Owner's Agent, returned to her, and a wire was run out to seaward for a tug to pick up. It was hoped to tow her off at high tide, but as the tide rose the wind went round to the eastward and freshened. The sea got up rapidly and the 'Saltaire' was swung broadside on to the seas and fell over to seaward. She lay at an angle of 40 degrees with the seas breaking right over her. Her crew took shelter in the wheelhouse. The lifeboat crew had been watching and they launched at once, it was then 2pm.

There was not enough water betweeen the 'Saltaire' and the shore for the lifeboat to get to leeward of her, and on the windward side it was impossible to approach because, lying at an angle as she was, her masts were in the way. The only way to rescue her was to haul them through the water in a breeches buoy. The Coxswain anchored to windward, paid out a little cable, made fast another rope to the cable from the starboard quarter, and then by going ahead and astern on his engines, he kept the ropes taut and held the lifeboat steady while a line was fired over the wreck. A tail block and a lifebuoy from the lifeboat were then hauled across by the trawler's crew but they had very great difficulty in finding a point sufficiently high for fastening the block.

In the end, with the seas breaking over them, they succeeded in making it fast to the top of the wheelhouse. Then came another difficulty, to get into the buoy with the deck at so sharp an angle and the seas smashing over it. Three of the men had succeeded and had been hauled through the surf to the lifeboat, when some nets and other gear were washed out of the trawler and fouled the ropes and buoy. Another line was fired and another block sent over to the wreck and made fast. Then the work of rescue began again and another 4 men were hauled into the lifeboat, but 3 were still on the wreck.

It was now over an hour since the lifeboat had anchored. The strong flood tide, the wind blowing across the tide, the shallow water, the heavy seas - all this made it extraordinarily difficult to keep the lifeboat close enough to the wreck for the buoy to be drawn backwards and forwards and at the same time to prevent the lifeboat from being flung on to her.

At times they were 30 yards apart, at times nearly touching, but the Coxswain was most skilful in handling the lifeboat and his crew most skilful in working the buoy through the breaking seas and hauling the men aboard the lifeboat. It was proof of their skill that not one of the 7 men was hurt, but the other 3, who for over an hour had watched their comrades being hauled through the seas, could not face it themselves. They preferred to be rescued from the shore and a party of soldiers hauled them through the surf. Two of them were badly hurt. At 3.30

the lifeboat left the wreck and twenty minutes later was landing the rescued men.

The Institution made the following awards:-

To Coxswain Robert Cross, a second clasp to his Silver Medal for Gallantry, a copy of the vote inscribed on Vellum and £5;

to John S. Major, the Motor Mechanic, the Bronze Medal for Gallantry, a copy of the vote inscribed on Vellum and £5;

to each of the other 6 members of the lifeboat crew, Second Coxswain William R. Jenkinson; William J. T. Hood; Bowman Samuel Cross; Assistant Motor Mechanic Samuel F. Hoopell; George F. Hooper and Walter Biglin, the thanks of the Institution inscribed on Vellum and £5.

Permanent paid crew, Standard rewards, £1 7s; special rewards £40, total rewards. £41/7s.

Just before 8am in the evening of January 6th 1943, the Humber Lifeboat Station received a request from the Extended Defence Officer for the Lifeboat to go to the help of Phillips Defence Unit No.1, which was reported to have gone ashore inside the boom defence on the north side of Trinity Sands.

The motor lifeboat 'City of Bradford II' was launched at 8.10pm. It was then blowing a full gale from the east against a strong ebb tide. The night was heavily overcast and very dark and there were frequent snow showers. The lifeboat passed the gate in the Boom Defence 19 minutes after launching and the boom defence vessel, which was connected by telephone to the shore, called to her by megaphone that a tug had gone to the help of the Phillips Defence Unit so the lifeboat returned to her Station at 8.35pm.

But no sooner had she been housed than word came to the Coxswain that a vessel was aground on the Binks. As the tide was ebbing, the Coxswain knew that he could not approach her and that she would lie quiet on the sands until the flood tide. He and his crew stood by.

Then at 10.50pm the Port War Signal Station telephoned that Phillips Defence Unit No.3, had broken adrift from her moorings and was entangled on the inner side of the boom defence. From the lifeboat station the men on the Phillips Defence Unit were seen to be firing red rockets and making signals for help. They were in grave danger of being swept out to sea by the strong ebb tide. 10 minutes later the lifeboat was launched and found the Phillips Defence Unit now thoroughly entangled in the boom. The lifeboat approached from the seaward side by the light of searchlights from the shore which, at times were of help to her and at other times blinded the crew. She approached the Boom bow on, she did this 4 times and the 5 men on the Phillips Defence Unit jumped aboard her. The lifeboat herself had her stem and bow planking damaged by the long steel spikes of the Boom, which were there expressly for sinking small boats. At 11.20 the lifeboat landed the rescued men at the lifeboat slipway and then tied up alongside a Patrol Vessel to wait for the flood tide in order to go to the help of the vessel on the Binks.

At 3.10am the next morning the 'City of Bradford' cast off and found H.M. trawler 'Almondine' lying on her side on the sands. Her port side was under water and she was smothered with heavy seas. The night was still overcast and very dark and there were still heavy snow showers. A strong spring flood tide was now swirling over the Binks at a rate of 5 or 6 knots and the seas were breaking from all directions.

The 'Almondine' signalled the lifeboat and asked her to take off her crew. At 3.35am in the morning the Coxswain made the first attempt. He ran the lifeboat, head to tide, alongside the trawler's lee side and got a rope aboard her. The rope was secured but almost immediately a swirling tide swung the lifeboat round and the rope was broken and the lifeboat's mast fouled the trawler and was broken. With the breaking of the mast her wireless was put out of action.

The lifeboat again approached the 'Almondine'. She did so no fewer than 12 times, first from one end then from the other. She did it in swift dashes, remaining alongside just long enough for a man to jump off the stricken trawler onto the lifeboat, then sheering off again so as not to be smashed against the trawler's sunken side.

All the time the heavy seas were sweeping over her, they twisted and tossed her about at will and several times they hurled her against the mass of the trawler.

Five feet of her oak stem, already damaged against the boom in the earlier service that night, was splintered right back to the planking of the boat and the planking itself was holed just above the water line. Sometimes one man jumped, was grabbed, was dragged aboard, sometimes 3 men jumped at once. By 4.20am, 45 minutes after the first attempt, 19 men had been rescued in this way.

The tide was rising and as it rose the trawler seemed to be righting herself. She now seemed to be waterborne again and her Skipper hailed the lifeboat Coxswain to ask if he and his Officers should now abandon ship or remain aboard but before the Coxswain could reply, the trawler's lights went out and nothing more was seen of her in the darkness and driving snow.

By the help of the lifeboat's searchlight and the shore based searchlights, the Coxswain scoured the sandbanks and the entrance to the River Humber for an hour and a half. No sign of the 'Almondine' was found and the lifeboat returned to her Station at 6.15am, there the 19 men were landed and Coxswain Cross telephoned to the Port War Signal Station. To his amazement he was told that a tug had found the 'Almondine' drifting near the mouth of the Humber and had taken her in tow.

Though damaged, the lifeboat was still seaworthy, and 4 days later she went out, with her damaged stem, and rescued 8 lives from another vessel in distress.

The rescue of the men of the 'Almondine' had only been made possible by fine seamanship, and the RNLI made the following rewards:-

To Coxswain Robert Cross, G.M., a second service clasp to the Gold Medal for conspicuous Gallantry, which he already held, with a Copy of the Vote inscribed on Vellum.

To George Richards, Reserve Motor Mechanic, the Silver Medal for Gallantry, with a Copy of the Vote inscribed on Vellum.

To each of the 5 members of the crew, George Stephenson, Bowman; Samuel Cross, assistant Motor Mechanic, and William Major, Sidney Harman and George W. Shakesby, Lifeboatmen, the Bronze Medal for Gallantry, with a copy of the vote inscribed on

Vellum.

To the Coxswain and each on the 6 members of the crew, a special reward of £5.

The crew were permanent paid men, and the ordinary rewards to helpers amounted to £2-5-0d. Special rewards to crew £35, total rewards £37-5-0d.

The events concerning the Danish Steamer 'Sparta' and the Belgian Steamer 'Anna' on January 11th 1943

At about 8.30am on January 11th 1943, the Port War Signal Station reported that the Danish Steamer 'Sparta' was in difficulties and a second message was received shortly afterwards that the Belgian Steamer 'Anna' of Nieuport needed help at once. At 8.45am the motor lifeboat 'City of Bradford' was launched. A strong S.E. wind was blowing with a moderate sea. A mile north of No.5 Trinity buoy the lifeboat found the 'Anna', she had 10 men on board, including a Pilot and was bound laden from Newcastle to Goole. In the early morning in a dense fog she had been in collision with the 'Sparta' and had sustained severe damage. Her deck forward was now awash and the lifeboat rescued the crew of eight but the Captain and Pilot decided to stay on board as the Bridge and after part of the ship were still above water. The lifeboat landed the rescued men at Grimsby and then at the request of the Naval Authorities she went out again to look for the 'Sparta'. She could not find her and learnt later that the 'Sparta' was making for Goole and that she arrived safely.

The 'City of Bradford' went again to the 'Anna' and found that she was not needed but promised to return again as the tide rose and stand by until after high water. This she did, reaching the Steamer at 8pm, she found a Naval salvage party on board. The 'Sparta' had grounded and the salvage crew had pumped her out and on the high tide she refloated. She was taking water but the pumps were able to control the water. Assuring themselves that the 'Sparta' was in no further danger, the lifeboat returned to her Station, arriving at 11.15pm.

Permanent paid crew, rewards. First Service, 18/-; Second Service, Property salvage case.

The service accorded to the Steam Trawler 'Chandos'. April 22nd 1944

On April 22nd 1944, at 10.55pm the ever vigilant lifeboat watchman reported a vessel aground on the Binks. Shortly afterwards the vessel signalled SOS on her whistle. The weather was fine with a light variable wind and a smooth sea. At 11.20pm the motor lifeboat 'City of Bradford II' was launched and after searching the area found the steam trawler 'Chandos' of Grimsby with a crew of nine. She had run aground while returning home with a full hold of fish from the North Sea fishing grounds. She was lying close to a wreck and was in danger of driving on to it when the flood tide made.

Two members of the lifeboat crew went aboard the 'Chandos'. At low water the lifeboat had to stand off but as the tide made, she returned alongside again and ran out an anchor. With this help the trawler eventually refloated. When the 'Chandos' had come into the River the lifeboat took off her crew members and reached her Station again at 6.15am next morning.

Property salvage case. Permanent paid crew.

Events of 6th October 1964

Humber, Yorkshire. At 7.30am. On Tuesday 6th October 1964, the Nightwatchman reported that the reserve lifeboat 'The Cuttle', ON 833, appeared to be dragging her anchor in the rough seas and near gale force Westerly winds. At 7.50am the Station Lifeboat 'City of Bradford III' was launched. As it was over an hour past high water the combined effect of the wind, sea and tide was to break 'The Cuttle' from her moorings, and she was well out to sea in broken water before a tow line could be taken to her by the second Coxswain, who jumped from one lifeboat to the other.

Due to the bad conditions it was necessary to tow the reserve lifeboat into Grimsby, where she was moored safely at 11am. The 'City of Bradford III' stood by until the weather moderated. While she was there a message was received from a Shipping Agency saying that a man on board a vessel in Spurn Anchorage required medical attention. It was not until 3.45pm, however, that a male nurse arrived, as no Doctor could manage the trip at the time. At 5pm, the nurse was put aboard the cargo vessel SS 'Thorpe Grange' of London. The injured man was then transferred to the 'City of Bradford III' and was landed in the Royal Dock Basin in Grimsby at 6.35pm. The Humber Lifeboat then towed the 'Cuttle' to moorings in the Royal Dock and returned to her Station at Spurn the following morning.

The wreck of the Motor Vessel 'Anzio' aground off Donna Nook, Lincs.

At 11.40pm, on Saturday, 2nd April 1966, the Coxswain Superintendent at the Humber Lifeboat Station received information from the Humber Coastguard that two red flares had been sighted off the Lincolnshire coast in the direction of Donna Nook.

There was a strong gale from the north east and the weather was overcast with intermittent showers of heavy rain, the flood tide had been making for two hours.

At 11.50pm, the lifeboat 'City of Bradford III' was launched and proceeded. The wreck was sighted at 40 minutes past Midnight on 3rd April heading north west and lying with her starboard side beam on to the seas. Heavy seas were half way up the deck and washing right over her.

In view of the heavy, confused seas on the bank and around the wreck, the Coxswain decided to anchor and veer down to the casualty, since there was no possibility of being able to get alongside.

The anchor was let go at five minutes to one, and the Coxswain commenced to veer down. Whilst so engaged, the party tending the cable forward, consisting of second Coxswain Beverley, Bowman Staves and crew members Knaggs, were washed off their feet and back on to the wheelhouse by a heavy sea which completely enveloped the lifeboat. The second Coxswain was bruised whilst the Bowman received injuries to his ribs and Knaggs sustained head injuries. All three men immediately

returned to their Stations and continued to veer the cable until the lifeboat was within 30 yards of the 'Anzio'. Meanwhile the Breeches buoy and the gun line had been made ready for use.

Once in position to seaward of the wreck, the searchlight was trained on the 'Anzio'. And she was seen to be on her beam ends with nothing visible aboard. From the fact that 15 foot waves were washing right over her it seemed obvious that the crew had either abandoned ship or had been swept away. Coxswain Buchan nevertheless remained scanning the wreck in the beam of the searchlight for signs of life for a further 20 minutes before deciding that no useful purpose could be served by remaining longer.

During this period the seas, which were continually washing over the lifeboat, on three occasions completely filled the cockpit and after cabin. Having caused the plastic 'Doutarp' side screens to the wheelhouse to bulge inwards with the weight of water, both cockpit and cabin cleared rapidly on each occasion, the echo sounder was kept operating throughout and when veered down to the 'Anzio' the Coxswain had only 5 foot of water under his keel when in the trough.

Once the anchor had been recovered, the Coxswain continued searching down tide for survivors until 8.35am although convinced that any such search would prove fruitless in view of the fact that anyone would have been cast up on the beach by the onshore gale.

When the lifeboat left the vicinity all that could be seen was the mast and top of the funnels.

The lifeboat returned to her Station and rehoused at 9.55am on Sunday 3rd April.

At a meeting of the committee of management held on the 12th May 1966 it was considered that Coxswain Buchan showed courage and skill of a high order in approaching so close to the wreck under the weather conditions prevailing and that he was ably backed up by his crew. It was decided to grant the following additional awards:-

1. The Thanks of the Institution inscribed on Vellum to Coxswain R. Buchan.

2. Framed Letters of appreciation signed by the

Chairman of the Institution to the remaining members of the crew.

3. An additional monetary award of 50/- to all crew members including the Coxswain.

Silver Bravery Medal for Humber Lifeboat Coxswain re, Rescue of Crew of 'DIANA V'

Brian Bevan, Superintendent Coxswain of the Humber Lifeboat, was awarded the Silver Bravery Medal of the Royal National Lifeboat Institution for rescuing six people from a crippled Dutch freighter in the North Sea in December, 1978.

Just before the lifeboat reached the freighter it crashed down from a huge wave, putting out all the lights, so the rescue was carried out by torchlight from the lifeboat and a searchlight of a Warship. A 12 year old girl was the first to drop into the arms of a lifeboatman as the lifeboat came alongside the freighter, hampered by gale force winds, sub zero temperatures, snow storms and heavy seas. She was followed by a woman and 4 men who jumped to safety as the two boats were held together.

On the way to the rescue, two mechanics had to work in the engine room of the violently moving lifeboat to repair an oil pump. The mechanics, Barry Sayers and Ronald Sayers, second Coxswain Dennis Bailey and crew members Michael Storey, Peter Jordan and Dennis Bailey (Junior) were each awarded the Thanks of the RNLI inscribed on Vellum.

In an Official report of the rescue, Lieutenant Alan Tate, Inspector of Lifeboats for North East England, said "This was a very long, dangerous and involved service. The Coxswain showed remarkable seamanship, leadership and initiative and, together with his crew, outstanding courage in effecting a rescue during a strong easterly gale in icy conditions, at night, without lights and in a snowstorm".

A full account of the Rescue is as follows:-

"At 2pm on 30th December 1978, Humber Coastguard informed Lifeboat Superintendent Coxswain Brian Bevan that the Dutch Coaster 'Diana V' was in distress 74 miles off Spurn Head and the Lifeboat 'City of Bradford IV' was alerted. Cromer Lifeboat and the Warship HMS 'Lindisfarne' also set out for the casualty. Twenty five miles from Spurn Point, the Humber Lifeboat suddenly lost speed, due to a fractured oil pipe, and as the situation on board the 'Diana V' was improving and other vessels were helping, the lifeboat had to put into Grimsby Fish Docks to collect a replacement oil pipe but rather than remaining trapped in until the tide was right, the Coxswain decided to make repairs on the way in the confined space in the engine room to strip down the pump, and as the lifeboat put out to sea they replaced the fractured pipe. Gale force winds were buffeting the lifeboat throughout and the violent motion of the boat made their job extremely difficult.

As the lifeboat set out again, the situation aboard the 'Diana V' worsened and she started taking water. The lifeboat headed into the 25ft seas at full speed, taking a tremendous pounding and as she crashed down from an exceptionally large wave, all lighting failed. Before repairs could be made HMS 'Lindisfarne' reported that the lifeboat was urgently needed to take off the crew of the stricken ship.

The lifeboat arrived at 11pm to find the 'Diana V' listing heavily. Sea water was freezing on the lifeboat's deck and rails and the wind was gusting to 56 knots, Storm Force 11. The lifeboatmen went out onto the deck, fastened their lifelines and stood ready with only two hand torches to illuminate the scene. HMS 'Lindisfarne' then switched on her searchlight and the Coxswain edged his lifeboat forward. A breaking sea hit the stern of the coaster throwing it onto the lifeboat and ripping away part of the fender. On the second approach a wave lifted the lifeboat and drove it into the 'Diana V', taking away more of the protective fender. The third run in was more successful and as the Coxswain held his boat alongside, a 12 year old girl jumped into the arms of the lifeboatmen, a woman and 4 men quickly followed her with the lifeboatmen breaking their fall.

The Captain remained on the 'Diana V' and the coaster limped into the safety of the River Humber with the lifeboat and HMS 'Lindisfarne' escorting. The lifeboat finally returned to her Station after 13³/₄ hours on service.

The Commanding Officer of HMS 'Lindisfarne', Lieutenant Commander Morrow, RN, was sent a framed letter of Thanks signed Major General Ralph Farrant, Chairman of the RNLI, for his considerable assistance as on-scene Commander and his help in illuminating the casualty during the rescue.

Dated 5th March 1979.

The Saga of the rescue of the crew of the 'REVI' 13th February 1979

Just before midnight on February 13th 1979, Humber Coastguard informed the Superintendent Coxswain of the Humber Lifeboat, Brian Bevan, that the Panamanian freighter 'REVI' was in distress and taking water 30 miles north east of Spurn Light vessel.

The lifeboat 'City of Bradford IV' was alerted at 0015am on February 14th and proceeded at full speed. Leaving the River Humber she met huge seas, estimated at 35ft in height, and speed was reduced to 14 knots. At 0107 the casualty reported that he was slowly sinking and half an hour later the lifeboat arrived. The wind was now north easterly Force 10. It was exceptionally cold with snow showers and the freighter was being completely buried by the heavy seas. The British ship 'Deepstone' was standing by.

The Captain of the 'Revi' asked for two of his crew members to be taken off. This seemed impossible and when the Coxswain asked the freighter to stop to see how she behaved, heavy seas sweeping across her whole length made the danger to survivors and lifeboatmen too great for a rescue in that position. Coxswain Bevan asked the casualty to steer south at a slow speed, and his crew fastened their lifelines to the lifeboat's rails.

The lifeboat was edged in under the freighter's starboard quarter just as a huge wave hit the port quarter, completely covering the 'Revi's' stern and sending her crashing down towards the lifeboat's deck. The lifeboat's engines were put full astern to clear the freighter. After

a number of similar runs in, with the 'REVI' often rising 20 feet above the lifeboat's fore deck, the first crew member jumped to safety. After several more attempts the second man was safely taken off.

The Captain hoped to reach the River Humber but 5 minutes later decided that he and the Mate should abandon the freighter which was flooding and had a list of 45 degrees caused by the cargo shifting. The freighter was still being swept by heavy seas across her length as she lay broadside to the storm.

The lifeboat again came alongside the heaving deck of the 'REVI' and was swept away from the ship's side by a large breaking wave. The lifeboat was brought in close twelve times before the Mate could jump into the arms of the lifeboatmen. The bows of the 'REVI' were now almost submerged and the stern, clear of the water, was hanging above the lifeboat. The last survivor, the Captain, was hanging over the side of his vessel, ready to jump.

On the tenth attempt to get the Captain off, the stern of the the 'REVI' rose again 20ft in the air and began to crash down towards the lifeboat's foredeck where the crew were lashed to the rails with no chance of escape. The Coxswain rammed the throttle full stern and the lifeboat powerful engines pulled her clear of the casualty by inches. While the lifeboat prepared for another run in, the 'REVI' was completely covered by three successive seas and the Captain was feared lost. When the water finally cleared he could be seen hanging on to the stern rails.

The 'REVI' was now in immediate danger of rolling over so the Coxswain decided on a dash into the 'REVI' in a trough between two waves. The lifeboat was driven under the port quarter, striking the ship's stern but the Captain jumped and grabbed by the lifeboat crew as he nearly fell overboard again. Within 5 minutes the 'REVI' rolled over and sunk.

The survivors were taken to Grimsby and were landed at 0520. The lifeboat then returned to her Station.

An official RNLI report of the rescue stated, "The courage, seamanship and expertise required to carry out this remarkable night service in appalling storm conditions combined with snow and ice cold water constantly breaking over the crew, necessitating approximately 35 separate occasions of going alongside, was absolutely outstanding and in the very best traditions of the RNLI.

In additions, the leadership and initiative shown by Superintendent Coxswain Bevan was of the highest order and was clearly demonstrated by the confidence this crew showed in him, whilst they were in such great danger themselves on the foredeck with their lives completely in his hands throughout the rescue".

Dated 29th March 1979.

A Different Type of Rescue

Two Humber lifeboatmen, Peter Jordan and Dennis Bailey (Junior) have been awarded the Thanks of the Royal National Lifeboat Institution, inscribed on Vellum, for rescuing two people from mudbanks in the Humber Estuary last December. One of the survivors had an artificial leg and had to be carried across the mud to safety on a night when Force 6 winds and snow showers added to the problems of the rescuers.

In an official report of the rescue, the Inspector of Lifeboats for North East England, Lieutenant Alan Tate, singled out the lifeboatmen's courage and expert seamanship and commended their effort and tenacity in the recovery of the 2 casualties.

The rescue was carried out using the inflatable boat from the Humber Lifeboat and Coxswain Brian Bevan and the other members of his crew received a letter of thanks from Rear Admiral Graham, Director of the RNLI, for their skill and teamwork shown during the rescue.

A full account of the Rescue follows:-

On the evening of 6th December 1980, a report was received that red flares had been sighted in the Humber Estuary near Immingham and at 2019 the relief lifeboat 'Edith Emilie' on duty in the Humber set out into a Force 6 north westerly winds and heavy snow showers. The temperature was below freezing. An hour later the lifeboat arrived on the scene and witin minutes the casualty, a converted ship's lifeboat which was aground on a mud bank, was picked up by the searchlight. An inflatable boat was lowered from the 'Edith Emilie' and crew members Peter Jordan and Dennis Bailey (junior) volunteered to crew her. The sea was choppy as they set off and when they reached the shallow water they had to haul the boat 100 yards through the water and onto the mud. The crew then walked another 100 yards through the mud which was very difficult as they sank into the mud every step. The lifeboatmen discovered that the survivors were suffering from the cold and it was decided after consultation with the lifeboat Coxswain to take them back to the lifeboat.

One man had an artificial leg and although he weighed over 12 stones, Dennis Bailey took him on his back and with Peter Jordan steadying him and shining the torch ahead they started out. Every step was a strain as the men sank into the cloying mud and they reached the inflatable in a state of exhaustion. The inflatable was relaunched and Peter Jordan took the first survivor to the lifeboat. He then returned to pick the second man up and Dennis Bailey and all three went back to the 'Edith Emilie'. The inflatable's crew had now spent an hour and twenty minutes in freezing conditions and were wet through, covered in mud and very cold.

The Coxswain then used his considerable skill and local knowledge to clear the shoal area, with mud banks dry on both sides of the lifeboat and with only 5 feet of water under the boat in places.

The casualties were landed at Spurn Point at 0125 and at 0138 the lifeboat was reported moored, refuelled and ready for service.

Dated 1st May 1981.

CHAPTER SEVEN

THE LIFEBOATS

On August 17th 1868, the Cleethorpes lifeboat named 'Manchester Unity' after the Independent Order of Oddfellows' subsidiary the Manchester Unity Friendly Society arrived at Cleethorpes, and thus began the relationship between the RNLI and the Port of Grimsby and the seaside resort of Cleethorpes.

The lifeboat measured 33ft by 8ft 6 inches and 12 oars were supplied to row the stoutly constructed craft that had been built by James Woolf and Son at Shadwell in London.

This first lifeboat based at Cleethorpes was very successful during the 14 years that Cleethorpes had a resident lifeboat, rescuing 35 lives and being launched 24 times on service.

In 1882, the Cleethorpes Lifeboat Station closed down and the whole operation was transferred, lock, stock and barrel to the Royal Dock Basin in Grimsby, a move deemed necessary by the RNLI for better facilities and ease of access.

However, in 1887, the RNLI retired the craft. She had served 19 years, in which she had given satisfaction but time was necessary to bring another lifeboat, more up to date and in keeping with the developing nature of the RNLI.

The next lifeboat was also called 'Manchester Unity' with agreement being sought from the Independent Order of Oddfellows and she was 38ft long by 9ft beam. She had been built by Forrest at a cost of £624 and she was based at Grimsby for 7 years, going out on service 5 times but did not rescue. On November 18th 1893, the 'Manchester Unity' sustained considerable damage while trying to get out of the Dock Basin to go to the assistance of a vessel in distress. Amid heavy seas and a full gale the lifeboat was flung against the wooden piles of the jetty and pier and was taken out of service and sent to the RNLI Storeyard in London for examination and repairs. A reserve lifeboat was sent to Grimsby to replace her.

The new arrival was known as 'Reserve No. 3'. She was a self righting craft measuring 38ft long by 9ft beam and she had been built by Livie Bros. in 1890. The crew liked her better than the Grimsby boat and when the report came from the RNLI that the 'Manchester Unity' was too badly damaged for economical repair, the crew were pleased to learn that the 'Reserve No.3' was to stay in Grimsby permanently and the Oddfellows gave permission for her to be named 'Manchester Unity'.

The third Manchester Unity was based at Grimsby for 10 years and she was launched to assist 4 times without rescue, then she was withdrawn into the RNLI reserve fleet. In 1901, when the Spurn Station were having a replacement boat built, the 'Manchester Unity' was sent to Spurn and she remained there until January 1903 when she came back to Grimsby until June 1904 when she was replaced by a new 'Liverpool' class boat which was named the 'Charles Burton' after the late Charles T. M. Burton, who had left the RNLI a large legacy. The 'Charles Burton' was non self righting but had a shallow draft which was considered useful for the Humber area. She had a sail and 10 oars and measured 38ft long by 10ft 9 inches beam. She was a popular boat and during her 23 years stay was called out on service 16 times and rescued 7 lives.

The RNLI's experimental steam powered lifeboat 'James Stevens No.3', which had been constructed by Messrs. J. S. White at Cowes, Isle of Wight at a cost of £3,298, was sent to Grimsby in October 1898. She was measured at 56ft 6 inches long by 14ft beam and she displaced 32 tons and was powered by a single 180hp Compound Steam Engine. On trials in the Solent she reached a maximum speed of $8\frac{1}{2}$ knots. This vessel was donated to the RNLI by the Trustees of the estate of the late Mr. J. Stevens of Birmingham.

The vessel was one of a class of 6 vessels built for evaluation and experiment by the RNLI. She was the only one to be propellor driven, the others were driven by water jets.

The 'James Stevens No.3' was stationed in the Royal Dock Basin at Grimsby for 5 years and she was called out on service 6 times but she was not to save any lives.

As with every experimental vessel, difficulties were found. She took at least half an hour to raise steam and she consumed an awful lot of coal, keeping two firemen busy. She also employed two engineers. She had a metal hull and really was a lifeboat in name only, her rakish outline with the two thin funnels side by side was impressive but her availability and size was not so well received. She was, of course, permanently moored in the Royal Dock Basin and actually was used more as a 'back up' facility for the conventional lifeboat 'Charles Burton'. She left Grimsby in January 1903 to go to Gorleston in Norfolk for further trials but she never returned to Grimsby.

When the 'Charles Burton' arrived at Grimsby, a new boathouse and roller slipway had been constructed to accommodate the new boat at a cost of £1,044. The 'Charles Burton' was to remain at Grimsby for 23 years in which she had been called out to assist ships in trouble 16 times and she had rescued 7 lives.

In 1927 the RNLI decided that the Grimsby Lifeboat Station was surplus to requirement and that the Lifeboat Station and whole operation should be concentrated at Spurn. So ended the Grimsby/Cleethorpes lifeboat operation which had performed a notable contribution to mariners in the South Humber area for 45 years.

Lifeboats at Spurn

At Spurn in 1911, when the RNLI at last took over the operation of the Lifeboat Station, the existing lifeboat was inherited from Hull Trinity House. This vessel was used until 1913 when it was replaced by an RNLI boat drawn from their reserve fleet. Not much is known about the old Trinity House lifeboat but it was presumably one of the 'Liverpool' type, shallow draught and non self-righting. The RNLI continued to use it for 18 months until one of the RNLI's boats became available.

In the summer of 1913 the new lifeboat arrived. She was named 'Charles Deere James', otherwise known to the RNLI as 'Reserve Boat No.9'. She was 'Liverpool' type, same as the old Trinity House craft, fairly old, being built in 1903 but she gave good service, being called out at Spurn 34 times and rescuing 32 lives. She was at Spurn for 6 years, after which she was returned to the reserve fleet.

After the departure of the 'Charles Deere James' in 1919, a new era of lifeboats began at Spurn. A motor lifeboat was sent to Spurn, of the latest type and embodying the most modern equipment, the crew were delighted and Coxswain Cross was very proud!

The name of the vessel was 'Samuel Oakes', the name being derived from a legacy of the late Mrs. E. M. Laing of Barnes, London. The new lifeboat had cost £7,156. She measured 40ft by 11ft beam and she had a 45hp Tylor petrol engine which gave a maximum speed of just over 7 knots. The 'Samuel Oakes' served at Spurn for 4 years and was launched 33 times and saved 25 lives.

Then followed the beginning of the 'City of Bradford' era. When the next lifeboat to be allocated to Spurn was donated by the 'City of Bradford Lifeboat Fund' in 1923, it was natural that the new vessel should bear the aforementioned name of that City. She was brand new and had cost £12,758 to construct, having every modern facility that modern lifeboat design could offer in the standard type of 'Watson' class of boat. This vessel served at Spurn for 9 years and was replaced in 1932, having been launched 36 times for service and rescuing 37 lives.

In fact the 'City of Bradford I' was complemented in 1929 by a new boat carrying on the 'City of Bradford' tradition, as 'City of Bradford II'. This 'Watson' class boat was the result of a donation from the legacy of Mr. Moss Howson and the 'City of Bradford' Lifeboat Fund. Strangely enough, she cost less to build than the older boat, £8,662. She was to serve together with her older namesake for $2\frac{1}{2}$ years. One assumes that the older boat being housed in the lifeboat house and the newer boat being moored.

The 'City of Bradford I' was withdrawn from service

The naming ceremony of 'City of Bradford II' lifeboat at Bridlington. Photopress of London.

in 1932, having given very reliable service when being called out in conjunction with her sister vessel.

The later lifeboat went on to serve throughout the Second World War, when she and her crews had many nasty moments. If ever a lifeboat survived all manners of tribulations, this lifeboat had them all. She suffered severe damage on several occasions and when she was finally withdrawn from service to a well earned retirement she had performed 228 call outs and had rescued 305 lives.

In 1954 a new boat, which was the gift of the City of Bradford Lifeboat Fund, was delivered to Spurn to be named 'City of Bradfoard III'. She again was a 'Watson' Class boat measuring 46ft 9 inches long by 12ft 9 inch beam. She was fitted with 2 FERRY VE4 Diesels driving twin screws and she had the most sophisticated equipment of the day.

She was capable of a top speed of $8^1/_2$ knots and had

a range of approx. 170 nautical miles.

This vessel served at Spurn for 23 years and was the last lifeboat to use the lifeboat house at Spurn. She was launched to service 351 times and rescued 107 lives.

In 1977 she was withdrawn from service and replaced by a totally different type of lifeboat, also bearing the name 'City of Bradford'. This vessel was an 'ARUN' class vessel and was the fourth 'City of Bradford' to be stationed at Spurn. She, too, was provided by the 'City of Bradford' Lifeboat Fund, plus the Sheffield Lifeboat Fund and the International Transport Workers Federation and numerous bequests. She was 54ft long by 17ft beam. She displaced 32-38 tons and was fitted with 2 'Caterpillar' Diesels which gave her a top speed of 18-4 knots and a range of 227 miles. She was built by Halmatic Ltd. in 1976.

During her 10 years service at Spurn, she was called out 416 times and rescued 106 lives.

This vessel cost £163,453 in 1976, a staggering figure but reflecting the colossal expenditure necessary to maintain the highest standards of the RNLI. She was of course, permanently moored off the Pilot's Pier at Spurn.

The present lifeboat at Spurn is another 'ARUN' class vessel. Although the 'ARUN' design has changed slightly, the new boat is 2ft shorter than her predecessor, named 'Kenneth Thelwall' in memory of the late Mr. Kenneth Thelwall of Walkington near Hull. She differs from the earlier 'ARUN' class by a slightly increased range, (234 nautical miles) and slightly more power from the 'CATERPILLAR' diesels. Her top speed is just over 18 knots and cruising speed of 16 knots and she uses 66 gallons of fuel per hour at full speed.

The 'Kenneth Thelwall' gives the Humber Lifeboat Station at Spurn a first class vessel which can cope with any type of distress call in almost any weather condition. Manned, still with a permanent crew and a Superintendent Coxswain, this lifeboat is well known nationwide for continual feats of rescue and the saving of life from a holidaymaker on his surfboard, who has become becalmed with the shore rapidly receding, to the injured man on a Super Tanker who needs immediate attention. In adverse weather conditions, the Humber Lifeboat, tiny in comparison to the vessels that it attempts to assist, nevertheless will be there. Sometimes, throwing from wave to wave but doggedly making progress to reach the ship in distress. The determination and courage of her crew will overcome most obstacles and continue to promote the name of the RNLI and the envied name of the Humber Lifeboat Station.

RNLI Humber Lifeboat 'City of Bradford III' in the Royal Dock, Grimsby,
in August 1970 undergoing stability tests after the fitting of new radar equipment.
Grimsby Evening Telegraph.

Royal National Lifeboat Institution
Bradford Branch

Seven lifeboats of the RNLI have borne the name 'BRADFORD'.

The first BRADFORD cost £450.

The first three 'BRADFORDS' were built out of funds raised in Bradford.

The fourth, provided by the RNLI, was also called 'BRADFORD' in recognition of the City's generosity.

The first four 'BRADFORDS' were stationed at Ramsgate, near the dreaded Goodwin Sands between 1866 and 1905. In those forty years they rescued 897 lives.

The 5th boat 'City of Bradford I' was built out of a fund of £10,000 raised in Bradford in the years 1920-1922, half of it was collected by the Bradford Chamber of Commerce. The lifeboat was stationed at the Humber from 1923 to 1932. She rescued 92 lives, 37 whilst at the Humber and 55 in the reserve fleet.

The sixth boat, 'City of Bradford II' was built out of £4,808 raised by the City of Bradford and the Airedale and Wharfdale districts in 1926. To this was added a gift of £5,000 from the Trustees (Taylor Jeffery & Co., Bradford) of the late Mr. Moss Howson of Harrogate. The lifeboat was stationed at the Humber from 1929 until 1954 and rescued 305 lives. She was then stationed at Amble from 1954 to 1956 and went into the Reserve Fleet.

The seventh boat was named 'City of Bradford III'. The Bradford branch was anxious to continue its association with the Humber Lifeboat Station and because of this the Committee decided in January 1953 to give the name 'City of Bradford III' to the boat that was being built for this Station.

The new lifeboat reached her Station in January 1954. The cost of this boat was raised by the Bradford branch.

These are the special gifts which Bradford has made to the lifeboat service. In addition, for many years, its citizens contributed over £2,000 each year to the general funds of the service.

Report dated October 1957.

The Cleethorpes Vigilantes Inshore
Lifeboat Service

The Vigilantes Rescue service was formed by local businessmen on 2nd November 1969 to provide a full time facility to go to the aid of boats, people and anything in difficulties in or at sea in the Cleethorpes area.

The main reason that such a service was formed stemmed from the tragedy of a local lady who took children onto the beach on horses for the usual ride, a regular treat for children. Unfortunately, thick fog rolled in and the riders were cut off. In spite of exhaustive searches the Lady and 6 of her charges were drowned. Public opinion after this terrible incident demanded some action and so the Vigilantes were formed to keep a vigilant eye on the local beach and coastline.

The Vigilantes are a voluntary body entirely and offers support to the local authorities, e.g. Police, the Local Council, the Coastguards and other public services. As mentioned earlier local businessmen realised that there was a need for such an organisation that would perform a multi-purpose operation such as going to the aide of small boats that drift around and people who disregard the basics of common sense and get into trouble with surf boards and airbeds. The Vigilantes undertake all manner of beach searches, digging out vehicles that have been stranded by the tide. In fact this body of people will tackle almost any call for help.

It must be remembered that the big lifeboat at Spurn is available as a back up for the Vigilantes and the degree of cooperation between the RNLI and the Vigilantes is one of respect and mutual trust.

Some of the members of the Vigilantes work for Cleethorpes Borough Council such as Bob Kaye, Brian Beckett and Frank Priest and are usually available at short notice. The other members on the active list give precedence to the Vigilantes in their spare time.

Prominent local people in the early days of the Vigilantes were R. Darnell, J. Oslear, R. Nicholson and many other public spirited men who wished to see a rescue service used to save lives in and around the resort.

Other ways that the Vigilantes give their services are

The naming ceremony of the present Humber Lifeboat Arun Class 'Kenneth Thelwall' was carried out on September 19th 1987 in Hull Marina.

Unique picture of the outgoing Humber Lifeboat 'City of Bradford IV' and the new lifeboat 'Kenneth Thelwall' (right) together with the Cleethorpes Inshore Lifeboat attending, the yacht 'Marique' which was in difficulty. 13th August 1987.
Grimsby Evening Telegraph.

RNLI 'City of Bradford II',
former Humber Lifeboat, in Dunbar
Harbour, East Lothian, 1963.
Withdrawn from service in 1968.
Bradford Telegraph and Argus.

RNLI Humber Lifeboat 'City of Bradford III' at Riverhead, Grimsby. Summer 1976.

Cleethorpes Vigilantes new Avon Sea Rider Inshore Rescue Boat.

in times of floods, relief to distressed seafarers who are in a shocked state owing to immersion for long periods in the water and many other ways this body of people try to perform wonders to an appreciative public.

The Vigilantes are based in a building behind the First Aid Station on Cleethorpes promenade opposite the Pier. Here the Searider craft is housed and is launched from the Pier Slipway.

Until the advent of the new Inshore RNLI craft 'TRICENTROL' in the Summer of 1988, the Vigilantes were under the control of the local Coastguards who relied upon them to attend local call outs in the Cleethorpes area. The Vigilantes never let anyone down and performed some heroic deeds of rescue and salvage. The large RNLI boat at Spurn would always be on hand if necessary. The admiration for the Vigilantes's service and dedication to duty is considerable and certainly their prowess is acknowledged by the men of the RNLI, even the ones among the RNLI who speak about "Men and Boys".

When the Vigilantes were first formed they were the only rescue local service in the area, (The RNLI had an inshore craft at Humberston until 1964 when it was withdrawn owing to lack of use), so the Coastguard would alert the Vigilantes for rescue if a distress call was received.

With the arrival of the new Inshore RNLI boat to be based in a purpose built unit next to the Coastguard Station near Brighton Street Slipway on Cleethorpes Promenade, it was assumed by many that the RNLI would completely take over the entire job of rescues and calls to assist people and boats in distress. However, this was not and certainly isn't the case. Admittedly the Coastguard will call out the RNLI inshore boat first but the Vigilantes have not been pushed out or forgotten in any way. They still perform a function and have a faithful following in the area.

Jobs like beach searches, digging out vehicles from the sand, and rescues at sea are still very much part of the Vigilantes variety of work.

The latest Vigilantes boat was brought into service in early November 1987 when an Avon Sea Rider Rescue craft was fitted with two way radio equipment and essential medical supplies to facilitate any rescue to be undertaken. This splendid boat cost in excess of £10,000 and was provided by donations and money raised purely by voluntary means.

It must be remembered that the Vigilantes have been called out many hundreds of times in fact the number of times now approaches 1,000. A tribute to the character and dedication to the task in hand could be illustrated by a letter published in the Grimsby Evening Telegraph of 29th November 1988 from a person named G. A. Clark of Grimsby.

The letter read as follows:-

"I decided to put pen to paper to congratulate the rescue services of Cleethorpes on what a fine job they are doing.

While walking my dogs along the sea wall, I spotted a fishing boat being washed towards the sea wall in the rough weather. No sooner had I seen it than I saw the Cleethorpes inshore rescue boat speeding towards it. They attached a line and soon began towing the boat in the direction of the fish docks. I watched for a while then continued my walk along the seafront.

As I reached the Pier, I saw some more RNLI Volunteers and the Coastguard looking out to sea. Wondering what they were watching, I stopped to see the object of their attention. I was told by another onlooker that a small boat was being washed along the tide line and it could be in danger. Soon the RNLI Volunteers ran across the road from the Cleethorpes Pier to where the Vigilantes Rescue Craft was kept and within minutes the Vigilantes craft was being hitched up to the Coastguards Land Rover. The boat was soon launched and sped out to the drifting boat and towed it to safety.

It was not until the rescue boats had returned that I learned that the Vigilantes Rescue boat had actually been manned by one Vigilante Member and two RNLI volunteers to save time".

Cleethorpes new Lifeboat House (Inshore) situated opposite Brighton Street Slipway. June 1989.

Brighton Street Slipway, Cleethorpes, always known as the Fisherman's Slip. June 1989.

This letter must show the teamwork of the Cleethorpes rescue services and how well they are organised to save time when necessary which could be critical in many cases.

So at least one member of the public is aware of the cooperation and mutual help that exists between the RNLI and the Vigilantes. Friendly rivalry no doubt exists but it would be strange if it didn't. The willingness to help each other in times of need is very refreshing and ensures that to anyone in distress at Cleethorpes that if it isn't the RNLI that speeds to your assistance in a fast inshore craft then a similar boat manned by volunteers of the Vigilantes will appear very promptly.

Details of some of the many rescues undertaken by the Vigilantes will give some idea of the variety and diverse nature of the call out procedure which was always began by a call from the local Coastguard:-

The fishing vessel 'Osprey' which had run out of diesel fuel $\frac{1}{4}$ mile off No.55 buoy in the river. The Vigilantes answered the call from the Coastguard and went alongside the fishing vessel and tried to start the engine without success, called Coastguard to advise of situation. Coastguard replied that Humber Lifeboat was on its way to assist. Vigilantes therefore returned to station and Humber Lifeboat towed the 'Osprey' into Royal Dock Basin at Grimsby.

Another call was to go to the assistance of people in water near Immingham, only to find on arrival that people had been picked up by small boats. A fruitless call maybe but all in the days work and at least they had gone out to rescue.

Request from Cleethorpes Coastguard to go to Immingham to escort 27' cabin cruiser to Grimsby. This boat had engine trouble and a lady on board in a distressed state. When arrived at Immingham observed that the cabin cruiser 'ALF ONE' under tow by motor fishing vessel 'ATHABASCA'. A member of the Vigilantes boat boarded the 'ATHABASCA' to offer help to the lady as she had also trapped her leg between two craft. He radioed Coastguard to ask for ambulance to be at Royal

Dock Basin as they were bringing in the lady.

Picking out some details of call outs from the log kept by the Vigilantes to record their details of their activities.

Here is one:- "Launched to assist in refloating 'BARBELLA' (80ft Coble Fishing boat) on Sandbank at the back of the day chalets at Humberston but we had to return to station following breakage of steering gear. Fishing vessel refloated by towing off bank using another boat named 'SCORPION' which belonged to member of Vigilantes crew.

Report of people on Haile Sand and Fort. Crew called out and boat launched to collect 2 people from Fort. Returned to Pier with these men who had ventured out to the Fort in a rubber dinghy and it had punctured so they couldn't get back to shore. Coastguard informed.

Request by Coastguard to go to assistance of 20ft fishing vessel (Converted lifeboat) 'EMMA LOUISE', broken down $2\frac{1}{2}$ miles east of fish docks. We stood by 'EMMA LOUISE' and awaited further instructions from Humber Coastguard. They radioed and instructed us to stand by near Bull Fort to meet Humber Lifeboat and slip tow with 'SEARIDER' which was a divers boat. Dropped divers boat near sewage outfall. 'SEARIDER I' towed into Cleethorpes.

We look at the case of 3 people rowing against the tide $\frac{1}{2}$ mile off the sewage outfall in a glass fibre hulled boat. The engine had stopped, apparently drive chain had snapped. Stood by until engine repaired by member of Vigilantes crew and then escorted boat to creek at Humberston.

Cleethorpes Coastguard alerted Vigilantes to go to aid of small inflatable boat with broken down outboard, drifting out to sea from Brighton Street, 2 people on board. People on board turned out to be Father and Son, both wearing thin T shirts and trousers. They were very cold and they had no anchor. One lifejacket between them, no flares and they were approx. a mile offshore when found by the Vigilantes.

During the years that the Vigilantes were the only rescue service available at Cleethorpes, they answered every call for assistance, in the most appalling weather conditions. They had placed themselves under the guidance of the local Coastguard and were available at all times. They attended a wide variety of calls, too many to enumerate but the fact is that this body of men, all volunteers, unpaid and from many walks of life, became the one lifeline to a careless surfboard rider, an ill equipped budding yachtsman, an adventurous swimmer who gets out of his depth and many other reasons why a call for help is heard or frantic signals are spotted by the Coastguards or other observant people.

One cannot thank the Vigilantes enough for their services, and it is to be hoped that the fortunate people picked up and administered to by the Vigilantes show their appreciation in the usual way. This way the Vigilantes can carry on with their good work and are able to attend other requests for help in the unexpected variety of tasks.

As I have mentioned before, the advent of the new Avon Searider boat operated by the RNLI did not deter or threaten the existence of the Vigilantes. Their operation will carry on. They are still available, the will to save life is still as strong as ever. Their operations will change as needed. If necessary they will act as a back up to the RNLI and the ever present helicopter from Leconfield, but meanwhile, they will keep a weather eye on the tide and the currents. They know what to look for and expect. As an alternative form of rescue, or in some cases the only form of rescue, the Vigilantes have never let anyone down and can be relied on to answer any call of 'HELP'.

CHAPTER EIGHT

THREE NOTABLE COXSWAINS

Levi Stephenson

For the last 4 years of the lifeboat operation at Cleethorpes, the Coxswain of the 'Manchester Unity' was the redoubtable Levi Stephenson, who by his skills and knowledge of the coastline and the fickle nature of the moving sand and gravel banks was well equipped for such a reasonable job. Levi knew the vagaries of the currents, the shoals, and the sudden changing nature of the Humber Estuary that trapped so many ships and sent them to their doom. The unwary mariner had to beware of the unknown and not take any chances in this area.

Levi's courage and temperament enabled the rescue services performed by the lifeboat to be respected along the coast. He certainly left his indelible mark on the local scene and his likeness forms part of the current Cleethorpes Coat of Arms.

Levi had a facial disfigurement that flattened his nose into a grotesque shape, but he used this to good advantage as he took parties of trippers out in his boat 'Cambridge Lass' (Which many say was the first lifeboat in Cleethorpes). He would shout out "Come for a sail with Old Levi, the man with the Big Nose". Children would stare at the big man, not quite sure of the nose, but the twinkle in the eyes would allay their fears and his heart was a kind one.

Levi and the other fishermen sold their catches on the green shore at Cleethorpes and Levi and his partner Amos Appleyard (Another original Methodist family in Cleethorpes) often operated a knock about turn with backchat and good humoured banter to good effect. He also had a refreshment booth in Victoria Terrace near the station which did well with the passengers going to and from the station.

Levi Stephenson was a member of one of the original Methodist families like the Appleyards. He was born in July 1815, the year of Waterloo and the final defeat of Napoleon and the Hope for Peace in Europe and he was baptised on 11th August at 'OLD CLEE'. He enjoyed a healthy, normal childhood and adolescence learning the skills and methods of fishing from his Father.

On May 22nd 1837 at the age of 21, he married Martha Dishman. Levi by this time could write his name but his bride could only make her mark or cross.

Their first child was baptised in June 1838 when Levi was described as a 'Mariner'. The family settled down in a rented home in James Street, later to be called Middle Street and finally as named today, Wardall Street.

During the Stephenson's tenancy of this house, a terrible tragedy struck the family. A cholera epidemic spread through the area, 80 people died in 6 weeks. Martha succumbed to this dreadful disease. Worse was to follow, for his baby girl died 3 days later and 2 days later a daughter of 9 years also died.

Such a series of hammer blows hit Levi very hard and for a while he didn't want to see or speak to anybody such was his profound grief. He shut himself in the house only venturing out for the odd fishing trip and to get provisions. The banter and sparkle once very evident had gone and the bright blue eyes had become sunken and lack lustre.

Eventually with the help of his family and friends, he dragged himself out of the slough of despair and picked up the bits and pieces of life, slowly at first but gradually the companionship of his pals and the zest for life returned and took him into calmer waters. After a year or two Levi married again but this union was fated and this woman became deranged and took her life by hanging, another tragedy for Levi to overcome. Happily, he did remarry and a happy union was created and this spouse survived him.

In the middle years of the 1870's, Levi became a member of the Cleethorpes lifeboat crew and the operation of the lifeboat benefitted from his experience. A year or two later he was appointed Coxswain, a very popular appointment. This promotion came as no surprise to his friends, they knew the quality of this man.

Levi's appearance was unforgettable. His large nose and his shape set him apart from his fellows, he was a big man, raw boned, his weather beaten face and the huge misshapen probosis were not exactly missed, some regarded him as the typical 'Meggie', if there ever was such a creature!!!

Levi's dress was unusual but very practical. He wore 'Fearnough' knickers which were a kind of 'Bermuda' short only made of thick cloth. He never wore socks or boots so in all weathers his brown, sinewy limbs were exposed to the elements. He wore a multi coloured knitted cap of the approved 'Smuggler' type, and he always had a bright blue Guernsey.

Levi would have been the first to admit that he lived in an interesting time. During his association with the RNLI he had experienced the extremes of rowing a heavy lifeboat with his mates in the most atrocious weather, the frustrating time spent trying to catch a shire horse to make up the numbers to tow the lifeboat out to a launch in a howling gale; then the difficulties experienced in harnessing up and the back breaking manoeuvres trying to launch the boat; the fright of the horses when they were out of their depth dragging the heavy boat on its carriage; the strength sapping rowing, usually with the current but all the same extremely tiring in the worst weather; the relief when sight is gained of the wreck and the expectancy of the pitiful spectacle of her crew marooned up the mast frozen stiff and unable to help themselves. What a choice when a vessel was stranded, sometimes she would heel over and the crew would take to the masts or possible they would chance it and stay on deck fearing the mast would break off thus depositing them in the grey waters. Levi had seen it all. He would have time and time again experienced the difficulty of trying to get alongside a stranded vessel when the waves threw the lifeboat either onto the stricken ship or far away on the other side. Every rescue mission had its hairy moments and in those far off days when Levi and his crew were manning the 'Manchester Unity', they deserved special praise for their efforts.

He would experience the thrill of potential danger and adventure when the maroon went up with a bang on a cold winter's afternoon. He would make his way the short distance from his home in Wardall Street to the boathouse, many of the crew would be converging towards the lifeboat. They would all be apprehensive and a bit nervous until the boat was launched but first of all the horses had to be caught and harnessed up, then the crew would hitch up the horses to the carriage, get into the boat and hope the tide wasn't too far out and deep enough water to launch the boat from the carriage. Possible the weather wouldn't be too bad, it could change dramatically though off those sand banks. One never knew what was in store.

The Coxswain always tried to appear calm and fairly collected. Levi would be no exception, the men trusted him and he returned their faith. Sometimes owing to illness or other kinds of circumstances, one or two members of the crew were unavailable. Then a volunteer or two would have to be found, some of them were promising, some were just keen to go to a shipwreck for the hell of it.

The operation of the local RNLI committee was effective and raised much needed money for the RNLI, but Levi would not tolerate interference and it was not necessary. When such a competent Coxswain was in charge it was wise to leave well alone.

Levi's fishing trips continued and the 'Cambridge Lass' earned her keep as a fishing vessel and a pleasure boat. Fish now landed at Cleethorpes from the smacks was taken to Grimsby Fish Market by horse and cart. A small amount was sold on the green shore and the local booths. Overcrowding in the fishermens area of the resort was though to be the cause of the outbreak of cholera in 1854. Such were the conditions in Wardall Street that 14 people were sharing 3 beds, 80 folk died in Cleethorpes in 3 weeks.

Levi's beloved Martha was only 39 years old when she died of cholera. Cleanliness, in those days was of secondary importance.

He usually arrived first at the lifeboat house when the maroon went up. He could do anything the other crew members could accomplish and in the worst of the weather he would try to exert a calming influence on the pent up anxieties of the crew. His kind nature ensured that the horses were not abused when launching or receiving the boat. It was not easy to launch the boat from its carriage in the bad weather and Levi felt for the animals whose fright and struggles were a source of worry, but still the boat had to be launched and the stricken vessel had to be attended. In the appalling elements, the lifeboat, trying to row with the current, would be tossed around like a crazy thing, the crew unable to steer or exert any influence on the progress. Only crests of waves and the seemingly bottomless troughs seemed to be trying to drag the fragile craft to its doom.

Eventually, a lull would occur and the brawny arms of the rowers would take over command of the lifeboat and progress would resume to the scene of the grounded vessel and her pitiful crew marooned up her mast. Levi's skill in eventually getting alongside the wreck was admired and appreciated by the rescued men and his crew on the 'Manchester Unity'. The long tiring row home now laden down with 5 survivors huddled in the whaleback seemed an age but finally the green shore of home loomed out of the mist and relief was profound.

To be a member of a lifeboat crew in those days was a calling. The ever present dangers from the cruel seas and the atrocious weather conditions were to be feared and viewed with respect. The heavy oilskin frocks, sou'westers and sea boots guaranteed that if you were washed overboard you usually drowned because the weight of the clothes, plus the oilskins and boots would render any attempts to struggle or swim virtually impossible. Fortunately, not many members of lifeboat crews did fall or were washed overboard but the risk was always present and one took the greatest care. In many cases the turbulent seas gave no choice and such was the fury of the wind and waves no one stood a chance. That was where a calm disposition came in. If Levi was the Coxswain, he looked after the crew by keeping calm and steady, calling for volunteers to go aboard a wreck which could be listing alarmingly with three or four men clinging to the mast was a regular occurence and there was no lack of offers to go to the ship. This was a very dangerous risk getting from the lifeboat to the wreck and it was then that the crewman's life was in very great danger. Usually the manoeuvre was carried out successfully and the exhausted crew brought over to the lifeboat which was bobbing about like a cork. Again the problem of getting back onto the 'Manchester Unity' was easier said than done and the element of danger was never far away. However, at last the crew and survivors were transferred with a few cuts and bruises and the return journey home could begin.

When at last the lifeboat was pulled onto its carriage by the heavy horses the extent of damage to the lifeboat could be clearly seen. Several parts of the hull had been sprung, 2 oars had broken and about 3 inches of water was washing about in the bottom of the boat, but she had made it home and lived to go to a rescue another day.

The crew would stumble home exhausted, the rescued mariners would be attended to by a local Doctor and given accommodation for the night. Levi, after seeing that the lifeboat was tucked up, would wearily walk to his home in Wardall Street.

The coming of the lifeboat to Cleethorpes provided a coordinated operation which surpassed the previous eager, enthusiastic attempts by local fishermen to go to the attention of ships in distress. The shore boats, 'Deerhound' and 'Mariner's Friend' or more commonly known as Snatchall and Grabball, these two vessels were primarily after salvage money but insisted that saving lives first and salvage for vessels secondary. It was a unofficial race between the 'Manchester Unity' and these two shore boats and an air of disapproval was very apparent from the RNLI.

Levi's tenure as Coxswain of the 'Manchester Unity' ended in 1882 when the whole operation was moved to the Royal Dock Basin at Grimsby. Levi returned to his boat and relaxation, the 'Cambridge Lass' still had years of life in her but Levi was feeling his years and sat around mending his and other friend's nets and talking about old times.

In the Summer season, he was nearly always around, an unmistakable figure now slightly bent but the twinkle was still in the eye and the story was never far away.

Cleethorpes had lost its lifeboat and many regrets were expressed forcibly. Mr. E. Bannister, the Chairman of the local branch of the RNLI, had several letters demanding that the lifeboat should be reinstated but to no avail. The lifeboat had gone to Grimsby, a strange decision because of the tidal nature of the Dock Basin.

Levi would have been very impressed with the development of Cleethorpes which had grown in every direction. The coming of the Railway in 1863 helped and visitors flooded in from the Midlands and South Yorkshire, bringing prosperity and trade for the resort. His other interests, the Victoria terrace refreshment booth supplemented by a tea stall at the corner of Sea View Street had been very well established and were now run by the family.

His boat, the 'Cambridge Lass', was very popular being strongly associated with Levi 'The Famous Coxswain', whose fame had spread far and wide. Levi would smile at the stories of fame and shrug, he always would maintain that he was doing a job and if risk came into it so what, besides, his crew were also responsible for the successful results of the rescues, so they had to share the acclaim.

Coxswain Robert Cross, G.M. of the Humber

Coxswain Robert Cross joined the crew of the station at Spurn Head on the Humber on 11th October 1902, when the station was under the control of the Hull Trinity House. He served in it for 6 years, and then left and bought a share in a Herring Drifter.

In 1909 he went out with the lifeboat at Flamborough to the help of several Flamborough cobles caught in a sudden gale. Two of the cobles were lost, with one of them went down Coxswain Cross's brother and the brother's two sons. After this tragedy, Coxswain Cross decided to devote himself to the lifeboat service. The opportunity came 2 years later, when the RNLI took over the Spurn Point Station. Coxswain Cross then sold the fishing boat and returned to Spurn as Coxswain of the lifeboat.

There he remained as Coxswain for 31 years, retiring in November 1943 at his own request at the age of 67. During the War of 1939-1945 he had a finer record than any other Coxswain, winning the George Medal, The Institution's Gold Medal for outstanding Gallantry twice, its Silver Medal, its Bronze Medal and its Thanks on Vellum.

During these years of War he took part in the rescue of 244 lives. In his 31 years as Coxswain he rescued 403 lives and his complete record of awards for Gallantry is 2 Gold Medals, 1 Silver Medal, 2 Bronze, the Thanks on Vellum and last but not least the George Medal.

His grand total of lives rescued, including the 6 years in which he served as a crew member, totalled 453.

Brian Bevan, Second Man to win Gold Medal in 13 years

Brian Bevan, aged 32, Coxswain of the Humber Lifeboat, became the second man in 13 years to be awarded the Royal National Lifeboat Institution's Gold Medal for Gallantry, sometimes known as the Lifeboatmen's VC.

On the night of 14th February 1979, the Humber Lifeboat put out in a fierce force 10 gale with snowstorms and 35 foot waves to help a freighter which was sinking in the North Sea. Brian Bevan had to bring his lifeboat alongside the listing ship no less than 35 times before the crew of 4 could be rescued.

As he tried to take off the Captain, the freighter rose 20 feet above the lifeboat and began to crash down towards the lifeboat crew, who were lashed to the rails with no chance of escape. The Coxswain immediately put his engines hard astern and managed to pull clear by a few inches. The Captain disappeared under the waves but by driving the lifeboat in again, Brian Bevan saved him minutes before the freighter sank.

The other members of Brian Bevan's crew, Dennis Bailey, Barry Sayers, Ronald Sayers, Michael Storey, Peter Jordan, Sydney Rollinson, and Dennis Bailey (Junior) were each awarded the RNLI's Bronze Medal for Gallantry for their part in the rescue.

The last man to receive the RNLI's Gold Medal for

Brian Bevan at the helm of the 'City of Bradford IV' entering the Royal Dock Basin, Grimsby, in April 1979.
Grimsby Evening Telegraph.

Gallantry was Keith Bower, second Coxswain of the Torbay Lifeboat, for the rescue of 10 people from a freighter in December 1976.

Brian Bevan was awarded the RNLI's Silver Medal for Bravery for a rescue in December 1978 when six people were rescued from a crippled Dutch cargo vessel in appalling conditions.

He received both of his Medals from the Duke of Kent, President of the RNLI, at the Institution Annual presentation of awards held in May at the Royal Festival Hall, London. It was to be the first time anyone has been presented with a Gold and Silver Medals of the RNLI at the same meeting.

CHAPTER NINE

AT LAST, A VISIT TO SPURN

I had always promised myself a trip to Spurn, but like a lot of things, I put such an adventure off. However, as the story of 'Lifeboats of the Humber' progressed, I felt an urge to go to this desolate spot in such a vulnerable position which is only 6 miles from Cleethorpes near where I live but some 70 miles by road. I had imagined several times what Spurn would be like, and as I wrote the book I thought a certain amount of romance would bound to be around somewhere. After all I had been researching the history of the place for over two years so my mind was somewhat confused by the information contained in the material.

Also, I wanted to see for myself the exposed, wind swept, sand covered peninsula that had been part of my life and work for so long.

Apart from a few old photographs that didn't convey much of the present conditions, I was woefully ignorant of the life and times of this isolated, desolate settlement.

Spurn peninsula is now a nature reserve which is owned by the Yorkshire Naturalist Trust and is very important in the study of European bird migration, many species of birds of rare varieties are seen at Spurn.

The Trust bought the reserve in 1960 and this includes nearly all the area south of Kilnsea village, which amounts to nearly 280 acres of land above the high water mark, a further 480 acres of foreshore is also administered by the Trust.

Hull Trinity House leases from the Trust the small area on which the lighthouse stands. A full time Warden is employed by the Trust to look after things and to take

The two lighthouses and remains of Smeaton's circular lighthouse base with the cottage
within its walls at Spurn Point. October 1985.
Grimsby Evening Telegraph.

Spurn Point with its narrow spit of eroding land showing the two old lighthouses. March 1988.
Grimsby Evening Telegraph.

the money from visitors and advise on enquiries, thus enabling visitors to proceed towards the end of the peninsula.

One is very aware of the wild nature of the narrow spit of land that reaches out into the Humber Estuary. Sea buckthorn and marram grasses grow in profusion amid the ever moving dunes of fine insidious sand.

The day of my visit dawned bright and sunny and three of us piled into the car and enjoyed a pleasant journey throught the flat east Yorkshire countryside. We broke our journey at the 'Crown and Anchor' at Kilnsea where a very decent lunch was taken. The Inn has many photographs and memoribilia connected with Spurn and the lifeboat, and I regarded this as a taste of things to come.

Having enjoyed our food, we set off on the remaining $3^1/_2$ miles of narrow twisting mainly sand covered road to the end of the peninsula and the lifeboat station. Now we were in the middle of the narrowest part of the spit and

we could see quite clearly where the sea had broken across the narrow land and had almost succeeded in creating an Island.

The Spurn bight was showing its foreshore on our right and the North Sea was hurling spume over the newly created embankment on our left. The sea will reclaim its own and the purpose was very apparent, even the huge blocks of concrete that had been dumped into the gap were vulnerable on a high tide and a Force 9 Gale.

Sand had, in places, nearly covered the narrow road and passing places had to be used by motorists. We approached the now disused lighthouse, standing sentinel and reassuring in the dominant position, still in good repair and we assumed that it was a listed building. Its long abandoned mate was surrounded by water after having been used in the First World War as an explosives magazine.

About 150 yards from the tip of the peninsula we found a large car park where we left the car. At this point sands blow down from the sand hills covering the road and stinging faces with its fine particles. Now a strong wind had blown up and the temperature had dropped, we felt very exposed. We saw the remains of foundations of previous cottages. Exploring the sand hills revealed many abandoned ruins of First World War block houses, the memory of the fortifications so elaborately constructed to keep the German enemy at bay, the sinister remains of a concrete gun emplacement to house a 9-2 inch Coastal Gun, its range finder now part of the Pilot and Coastguard look out position.

Everywhere on Spurn Point, relics of both World Wars reminded one of the War time emergencies and what might have happened.

Today, the untidy remains do not hinder the Pilots, or the Coastguards or the operation of the RNLI Station. The present lifeboat, 'Kenneth Thelwell', is moored to her orange buoy just off the Pilots Pier. The boarding boat, so necessary, is moored to the dolphin for immediate use. The ochre coloured cottages built for the resident lifeboat crew are very noticeable, if only because of their contrasting colour.

Both lighthouses continue to dominate the scene, if only as memories of the powerful light that used to shine from their powerful lens. The dark grey concrete ruins of Spurn, now sand filled and trying to emphasise their use but of a different time, give the visitor plenty to think about on the way home.

Traces of the light railway are visible along the road from Kilnsea to Spurn. Built in the early part of this century, it ran from Kilnsea to Spurn, a matter of $3^3/_4$ miles amid the sand dunes and hills. It had a variety of small steam locomotives and an even stranger collection of diesel and petrol engine Railcars. The passenger carrying rolling stock was typically 'Colonel Stephens' in character and nature, very quaint but it served the useful purpose of conveying passengers and items to and from Spurn to Kilnsea and back.

This Railway closed about 1951-52 and it is remembered with affection to this day.

Walking around the sandy paths of Spurn Point, it is not difficult to imagine the place as it was in the early days of the lifeboat operation. To think of the generations of brave and durable men who had manned the first, cumbersome, heavy lifeboats in all weathers, to the present day.

I was given permission to walk on the Pilot's Pier to the end and view the 'Arun' class lifeboat at her moorings just off the end of the Pier. The wind had strengthened and I felt colder as I braced myself walking the exposed Pier. On my left, the now unused lifeboat house last used to house the Watson Class lifeboat 'City of Bradford III'. The present 'Arun' class boats could not possibly squeeze themselves into such a building. Nearby, is the old Admiralty Pier, which is still maintained, if only for the lights that are used for navigation purposes.

Looking back towards the land, one sees the white painted Pilot's premises, dating back to the old Barracks donated by the Chichester-Constables, the Coastguard-Pilot watch tower sharing the dominance of the settlement with the black and white banded lighthouse.

I stood on the T.Piece of the Pier, the wind gusting around me, the lifeboat bobbed easily at its moorings, the Pilot launch 'IDAS' bumped her mooring inside the Pier. What memories are evoked. Once can easily cast the mind back to the lifeboat crew digging stones out of the foreshore to ballast visiting vessels that took all their time, apart from manning the lifeboat. The cramped, damp, primitive cottages which were always wanting attention. Fresh water was obtained from the roof gutters and piped into a large underground tank from which it had to be pumped up by hand. During times of drought, water was rationed, each house being allowed one bucket of water per day. Sanitation was primitive to the extreme and involved chores. However, by 1933 the houses had been fitted with a sewage system which pumped the waste into the sea.

There were times when the sun shone and the wind dropped that Spurn took on a totally different guise. It could be described as quite pleasant, with sea practically surrounding the settlement. It is quite dramatic to see the sun rise over the North Sea to the East and to see it set on the Humber Estuary in the West.

Food and supplies in the old days were brought once

*RNLI boathouse at Spurn,
unused since departure of
'City of Bradford III' lifeboat.
To the right are the remains
of the Admiralty Jetty.
May 1989.*

*Lifeboat cottages at Spurn
with the children's play area
in the foreground.
May 1989.*

a week from Easington by horse and cart. Illumination was by oil lamps, there being no electricity or gas. Fuel for the fires was plentiful, driftwood was always available and considerable amounts of sea coal could be found, courtesy of the tides.

Routine maintenance of the lifeboat was an essential duty dating back to the first lifeboat establishment in 1810. The lifeboat had to be always available, so maintenance was absolutely essential. Latterly when motor powered vessels were introduced, a motor mechanic became a vital member of the crew, and the lifeboat had to be in condition for instant use.

The Humber (nee Spurn) lifeboat crew have always been employed full time and the men carry out a 24 hours watch. Today radar and other sophisticated equipment is linked to 100% surveillance but the human eye and ear are still very important.

Leisure time in the old days was somewhat limited in variety. The old Army tennis court near the old Railway Engine Shed (now demolished) was very popular. Swimming and fishing were popular pastimes, the men obviously knew where to swim from.

Gardening at Spurn is virtually impossible as the continually moving sand threatens to overwhelm plants of any kind.

It is assumed that today any leisure time is spent watching television or chatting to the neighbours, so a community spirit is apparent and one gets the impression of a closely knit community. The ever present possibility of a call out can happen at any time day or night, fair weather or foul.

The new cottages were built within the last 15 years and have been designed so as to make them as comforable as possible and as well insulated to keep at bay the extremes of the weather.

This desolate, windswept settlement has many memories of past lifeboat activities. The exhausted red eyed crew of the early pulling and sailing boats struggling ashore after a horrific night rescue; the stunned and dazed survivors of wrecks, brought ashore by the lifeboat; their emotional thanks to the Coxswain and Crew; their loss of personal belongings, unavoidable, but soul destroying; the grateful thanks of Master of vessels for advice and support by the Lifeboat standing by - again in all weathers, the subsequent refloating of the ship and the waves of goodbyes and thanks to the Cox; the rescues of frightened men and women by Breeches buoy, their gratitude also prolific.

The agonies of David Pye, the Coxswain in charge during the unpleasant stewardship of the Humber Conservancy Board (Mr. Pye was the man in the middle amid the threats of disestablishment and closure); the bullying, high handed methods used by the men in charge of the Humber Conservancy Board who should have known better; the continued bravery and leadership of Coxswain Robert Cross, whose record is an example to all; the no less achievements of the subsequent Coxswains, and the ongoing bravery and leadership of the present Superintendent Coxswain Brian Bevan who continues the great tradition expected of a Coxswain in charge of the Humber Lifeboat.

We are so lucky having a modern, up to date lifeboat and a dedicated crew who, will at all times, go out and attempt a rescue in the most appalling conditions.

Spurn Point has indeed seen it all. The bravery, the heartache, the gratitude, the threat to the lifeline of a narrow, sand choked road leading north, breached so many times in the past by the cruel sea, the ever possible fact that one day Spurn may become an Island. This threat is still very real.

Accepting that the RNLI are unique in the way that they are totally independent of Government assistance, and are a registered Charity, it is quite incredible to some people that this body still performs such a selfless, humane function, being called out to assist anyone in distress at sea. Often false alarms would stretch beyond all limits the patience of many, the RNLI would shrug their broad shoulders, smile and put such events down to experience.

The RNLI Inshore boat based at the Brighton Street Slipway in Cleethorpes, turns the clock back in so many ways for it was almost on the same spot that the first lifeboat house was built in 1868 and the original lifeboat 'Manchester Unity' was housed. So the operation contin-

The Spurn Lightship on station.
Town Docks Museum, Hull.

ues, apart from the additional fact that lifeboat operations today enjoy the assistance of the RAF Wessex Helicopter from Leconfield in Yorkshire that inevitably appears on the scene lending its considerable presence to the operation.

Combined Air-Sea Rescues are the order of the day in present times, and thus chances of saving lives are certainly better.

'Lifeboats of the Humber' has, I hope, enabled the story of a unique chapter in the saving of life at sea to be told, stemming from the first decade of the 19th century to the present day.

I have found the research and preparation for this material fascinating and very rewarding.

I have uncovered controversy and considerable conjecture which was totally unexpected and very surprising, the nature of man's reasoning completely unpredictable.

I feel the book had to be written if only to bring to light the story of 'Lifeboats of the Humber' as I think, it would seem that this collection of facts, so important to ALL that go down to the sea in ships, has remained relatively unknown for too long, and hopefully will now enlighten the general public who contribute so generously to the RNLI, as to the role of the only full time RNLI Lifeboat operation in the British Isles.

It has to be said that every boat that sails on the Humber or the Estuary is a potential lifeboat, in the way that a ship in trouble would attract help from any other boat in the area. Many lives are saved by ordinary people in ordinary craft and such is human nature that in these days, fortunately help of some kind is never far away, we hope . . . .

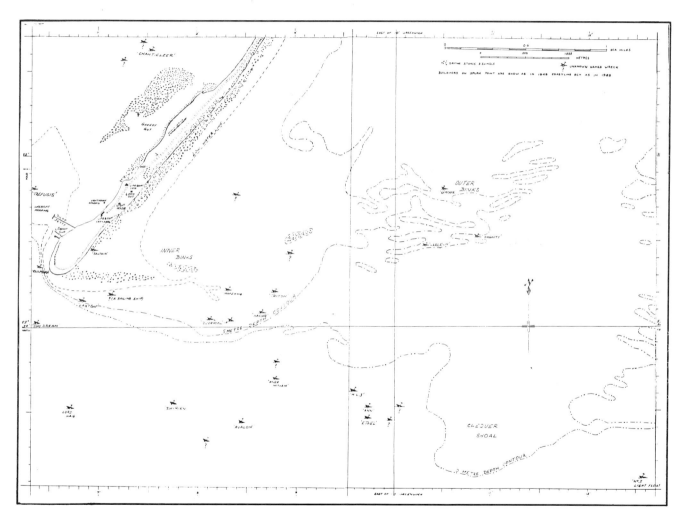

Chart of Spurn area showing positions of wrecks.